All I Want for Christmas Is My Two Tattoos

Patty Rodgers

All I Want for Christmas Is My Two Tattoos

Inspirational Stories from the Trauma of Diagnosis to the Drama of a Survivor's Dance

Patricia Beth Rodgers

All I Want for Christmas Is My Two Tattoos: Inspirational Stories from the Trauma of Diagnosis to the Drama of a Survivor's Dance

Copyright © 2008 Patricia Beth Rodgers. All rights reserved. No part of this book may be reproduced or retransmitted in any form or by any means without the written permission of the publisher.

Published by Wheatmark®
610 East Delano Street, Suite 104
Tucson, Arizona 85705 U.S.A.
www.wheatmark.com

International Standard Book Number: 978-1-60494-124-1
Library of Congress Control Number: 2008926537

Front cover art designed by Kellie Gower
Author's photograph by Sandy Watson

Written with sincere appreciation of the Scott & White Hospital in Temple, Texas, for early detection of my breast cancer, for the knowledgeable staff of professionals who guided me in making difficult choices in its elimination, and for the collective skills and prayers of the many doctors and technicians who treated my body as if it were that of a beautiful teenage girl.

Contents

Acknowledgements ix
Introduction xi

Chapter 1: Sharp Fangs of Fear 1
Chapter 2: Reason for Tomorrow 4
Chapter 3: No Place to Cry 8
Chapter 4: Journey of Trust 15
Chapter 5: Bargaining for the Baby 19
Chapter 6: Close, but Not the Purring Stage 23
Chapter 7: Seeking Cinderella 27
Chapter 8: Okay! I Got It! 32
Chapter 9: Snip, Snip 35
Chapter 10: Tunnels in Time: The Ant Lion 38
Chapter 11: Armor of the Arbor 43
Chapter 12: Gifts of Pink 52

Chapter 13: Got'cha 57
Chapter 14: One-Woman Parade 63
Chapter 15: Lost on a Clear, Bright, Sunshiny Day 68
Chapter 16: Devil at My Door 72
Chapter 17: Hopscotch & Dominoes 81
Chapter 18: Sunday's Hands 86
Chapter 19: Closet Secrets 93
Chapter 20: Perfect Center 98
Chapter 21: Wanted: One Baby Gorilla 101
Chapter 22: A Time to Dance 105
Chapter 23: Life's Sweet Frosting 109
Chapter 24: Stepping Out 117
Epilogue 126

Acknowledgements

I can not adequately express my thanks to the many people who prayed for me during my battle with breast cancer and who stood on the sidelines and cheered while I struggled through the real-life chapters in this book. First and foremost, I should thank Eddie, my husband and buddy, who demanded I take care of my health no matter how it altered my body. Although he often quietly questioned my sanity, he stood beside me through it all.

No book would have been produced without my Grandma Flossie encouraging me as a child to write, my mother Mildred's storytelling and editing skills, my sister, Stella Hunt, prodding me to write things that glorified God, and my two older brothers, Tommy and Douglas McWilliams, who provided me with enough fodder to fill many chapters.

Thanks to the women who allowed me access to their mailing addresses so I could send them samples of my work. What an encouragement it was that not a single one of them requested to be dropped from my mailing list while I struggled to find my voice.

Thanks to our friends and traveling companions, Billy and Linda Futrell, who provided us with many a mouth-watering meal when I was ill and who never fussed about the paperwork that accompanied us on vacations and had to be carried nightly into hotels along our routes. Friends such as these come along only once in a lifetime.

Others also helped: Kellie Frierson organized my manuscript and got me started in the right direction, and author, Susan Malone, plied me with heartening words and applied her expertise in editing. The charming poet, Peggy Zuleika Lynch, kept my head filled with encouragement every step of the way.

Lastly, I would like to extend a thank you to Sis Beck, Chairman of the Board and her daughter, Coleen Beck, President and CEO of Union State Bank. While other businesses were shy about hiring a woman fresh off the cancer-fighting trail, these two ladies welcomed me with open arms and provided me a platform to educate other women about breast cancer. They truly are, women helping women.

This book is written in memory of two friends who have already been called home and are celebrating their new cancer-free bodies in heaven, Linda Hopkins and Lee Galyean.

All I Want for Christmas is My Two Tattoos is dedicated to my beautiful daughter, Sharla Beth Williams, and Michael, Kevin, Mark, Stacy, Hud, ReGina, Rissa, Kathy and their children: Matthew, Taylor, Tyler, Peyton, Mason, Thomas, Lyndzey, Leah, Chandler and Abigail, for allowing me to be a part of their life. God has made me whole.

Introduction

The little girl had the making of a poet in her who, being told to be sure of her meaning before she spoke, said, "How can I know what I think till I see what I say?"
GRAHAM WALLAS 1858-1932

"There's one! Wait for me, okay?" I knew better than to pause for an answer. Always in a hurry, my husband, Eddie, had a hard time understanding why I would waste the extra minutes we'd shaved off of our trip to the clinic. He was mumbling something to the tune of "you're going to be late for your appointment!"

"Hello!" I said. "I like your pink hat!"

Glancing up from the magazine she was reading to pass the time away, a middle-aged woman greeted me with a smile. "It's to cover up my bald head!" Proudly removing it to show me a shiny pink scalp as bare as a baby's bottom, she turned her head from side-to-side.

"I must say, I had a closet full of noggin covers myself, but none as pretty as yours! I may have to find me one. I've become very found of the color pink after surviving breast cancer."

I had her full attention now. Plus, the lady to her left beamed brightly. "You had breast cancer? She does too! And chemo treatments? When? How long ago?"

Running my fingers through my thick head of hair I answered, "Long enough to grow my hair back in!" *But not long enough to forget how frightened I was when sitting in one of these chairs.*

In a few quick minutes, I recited the things breast-cancer survivors ask each other. The type and stage of your cancer when discovered, did you undergo a lumpectomy or a mastectomy, the number and pharmaceutical name of the chemo infusions administered, and most of all, the length of time it took your hair to start growing back in. My smile told her what she was probably too polite to ask; what were the results of my subsequent checkups and was I okay with my altered body?

She shared her medical facts with me. I promised to pray for her. Standing to leave, I gave her a bit of advice that helped me break the monotony of waiting for my hair to grow back in. "Ask your friend here to decorate the backside of your head once in awhile. With your pretty pink skin, I bet a bouquet of roses would be lovely peeking out from under your hat. I tried bull's eyes and pink hearts trimmed in red but my favorite was a happy face. I loved to pull my hat up from the back and smile at the person behind me in line at the grocery store. They're already staring at you and feeling sorry for you so why not lighten it up a little?"

"I've got to run. Good luck! I'll watch for you next time I'm here!" Patting her shoulder, I hurried toward Eddie standing close to the bank of elevators.

He had the call button pushed before I reached him. I let him fuss about the wasted time, knowing he wouldn't understand. Smiling to myself, I let the warmth of satisfaction wash over me, knowing I had kept the appointment God set forth for me before I arose to greet the morning.

Other people were bird watchers. I watched for bald-headed women! It wasn't hard to spot one. I looked for a hat, missing sideburns, and painted-on eyebrows. They came in all colors and sizes. Some were weak and some were strong. But they were always glad to see me, just as I had been glad to come across a survivor with an upbeat attitude. Who wanted to have a conversation with someone in the midst of making out her will? Not me!

I must admit I wasn't always this outgoing. Smiling came easy, but speaking to strangers was not my forte. Now, though, I understood a cancer patient's fears. I searched for opportunities to make them smile, to give them hope, to show them my hair. Producing a skit for cancer retreats, I persuaded others to help me present it. Together, as survivor sisters, we made the audience laugh, reminding them that the day we were diagnosed, we became survivors!

Other changes also occurred. Breast cancer made me face what was important and shed my worldly skin. Promoted by an angel named Renee Owens at the Scott & White Cancer Center, I began to write as I had never written before. Words poured through my fingers onto paper when I had the time. I discovered that all I had to do was sit before the computer and ask God for direction. My written voice began to develop into one I hoped others would like to hear.

Also, working to increase the profit line of a business no longer became my main purpose in life. Who, but my family waiting for me at home, would remember the nights I worked late or the Saturday's I spent at the office? There had to be a place where I could feel fulfilled, or at least an 8-to-5 job that I could walk away from each afternoon and still have the energy to write.

Serious though it was, the fear of cancer and the possible impromptu ending of my life, made me laugh as I had never laughed before. Tales from my youth ran zigzagged between the somber chapters concerning my fight with cancer. Memories of the taste of birds roasted on green sticks, face-to-face encounters with chicken snakes, the subsequent itch from the caging of chipmunks in my dresser drawer, all weaved their way into my story.

I wrote chapters of gratitude for my mother's comforting lap, my friends who stood beside me at work, God's granting of a plea made on my knees in a hospital's restroom, and even for my containment in a closet where I learned patience. Secrets walked onto stage and I acknowledged them with keystrokes, including those about old boyfriends, ex-wives, and my kidnapping by the strange man next door. For the first time since a long-ago childhood encounter, I revealed how I knew for sure Jesus didn't drink coffee! What a relief it was to put on paper the things I had kept quiet about for so long.

Medically, I was involved in making the choice to lose an entire breast or only have a lumpectomy. I had to decide whether to receive the recommended chemotherapy treatments and for the welfare of the women who would unwillingly follow in my cancer path, to decide if I wanted to join in a clinical trial. At the end of all the treatments, I had to make up my mind whether to undergo the many surgeries involved in the reconstruction of my chest, which included and concluded with two tattoos. All of these were life-altering decisions and yet, I had to face other major battles as well. Battles such as chasing away the evil force of the Devil to protect my family, bargaining with God for the life of my daughter's newborn baby, and finally, fighting to keep my job and most importantly, my health insurance.

I met my fears and survived them by drawing on the lifelong Christian strength depicted by my mother and my sister, by absorbing the strength offered by friends and other family members, and by allowing myself to relive my childhood as the little girl known as "Patty Cakes," who came to life and helped me face down my fears by continuously reminding me of earlier battles I had already fought and won. She portrayed herself as the tough little girl who survived the antics of her older brothers and carried me safely back in time to places where I could rest a spell.

My goal in recording my cancer experience was to capture my true emotions and preserve the story for others so they might be able to help their "sisters" or themselves through the scary experience of being diagnosed with breast cancer. Surprisingly, when I read the finished manuscript, I found a section of my backbone written into each of the chapters; making me realize for the first time how strong a woman I had become.

I hope you can find a quiet corner and travel with me as I discover the woman God expects all of us to be. Come join me in my search for a time to dance.

I did not write it. God wrote it.
I merely did His dictation.
HARRIET BEECHER STOWE 1811-1896

Chapter 1

Sharp Fangs of Fear

Never grow a wishbone, daughter, where a backbone ought to be.
                               — Clementine Paddleford

I hung up the phone and staggered to the office across the hall as if I had been shot. I still regret how I blurted out to Billie Jean, a friend I had worked beside for years, that I had breast cancer. I had no intention of scaring her as the doctor had just scared me. I remember Billie Jean saying in a shaky voice, "You'll be fine and your friends will be here to help you. You've proven before what a strong person you are and you can overcome this too." She was trying to be strong for me—lend me her strength but I knew that, like mine, her emotions were reeling.

Billie Jean's proclamation that I was a strong person seemed far-fetched. I could not remember a single time when I had acted like a superwoman in charge of my emotions. This situation was more than I could handle and the look of sheer terror on my face surely spoke louder than words.

My annual mammogram had detected a lump, and my doctor performed a biopsy. The phone call brought the worst possible news; the lump was malignant. Cancer was growing inside my right breast.

Stunned, I couldn't think. How was I ever going to make it through this? Where was this strength that Billie Jean thought I possessed? On that hot day in July, I began my long journey—a journey that was to be filled with the highest highs and the lowest lows.

That night I sat down at my home computer and let ugly words, typed in bold, uppercase print, declare to anyone brave enough to look over my shoulder, how angry I was at the world around me. "How" and "why," and their subsequent question marks, took up three-fourths of a page with the rest filled in with excuses of why I could not leave my family at this point in time. Feeling no relief, I backspaced over my tirade and shut down the computer. Seeking help, I called my sister, Stella, ten years my senior. She let me rant and rave and when I ran out of words, she let me cry. Then, very quietly, she suggested I get out my Bible and look for a verse that always made her feel better when fear raised its serpent's head and threatened to sink sharp fangs into her life.

Refusing to leave the bottom floor of despair, wallowing in a murky pool clearly marked "Why me?" I curtly asked her to read it to me, using the excuse that my Bible was not handy at the moment.

Speaking softly, with the confidence of someone who sought her Bible first in every scary situation, she said, "Maybe you should move it closer. I promise, reading it will help you get through this."

Jotting down the chapter and verse number, I half listened as she read. But later, when Eddie had gone to bed feeling helpless because he could not find words to comfort me, I stared at myself in the bathroom mirror. *I've upset enough people today, starting with sharing the doctor's phone call with Billie Jean this morning. Could I have handled that differently? And Eddie: most husbands would have found an excuse to leave the house after my crying fit, but he didn't. Poor thing, he doesn't have a clue how to make me feel better. I need to stop and think about how hard this is on him too. And, Stella. How rude was I today?*

Hanging my head in shame, I searched the house for my Bible. It wasn't lost, but it hadn't been moved from the spot where I had dropped it after returning from church last Sunday. Finding the verse, I read it over. Not feeling any comfort from the few words, I remembered Stella said to first ask God to give you understanding of what it was you were about to read. Bowing my head, I prayed in more of a demanding voice than God was used to hearing. The next time I read it, a quote from Franklin Delano Roosevelt popped into my mind, "The only thing we have to fear is fear itself."

Slowly repeating the Bible verse and the quote, I kept my head bowed and my eyes closed, giving myself time to absorb their truth. Finally, opening them, I noticed the room looked brighter. Had someone turned on another lamp? Knowing that wasn't possible, as sleeping Eddie was the only one at home, a smile threatened to turn up the corners of my mouth. Was it that easy? Did you simply ask for understanding of whatever lay before you and He gave it to you? What a novel idea! Is that how my sister painted with such beauty? Did she pray for God to guide her paintbrush? Would it work for writing? Could I ask for God's help and produce a beautifully written canvas of my own?

Looking in the bathroom mirror when I went to brush my teeth for bed, I saw a woman with hope-filled eyes smiling back at me. I debated on waking Eddie and letting him see my smile but knew he would only question my sanity. Tomorrow, I would show him the verse Stella had pointed out to me. For sure, he would like the end of it.

I couldn't wait to ask for help with my writing. First though, I better find out what God wanted in return. Maybe one had to be really in tune with His word before He would help with yours. At least, the topic of breast cancer hadn't monopolized all of my thoughts for the last hour. Relieved, I crawled into bed beside my snoring man. When he turned on the light in the morning, I hoped I would still be smiling.

> "For God did not give us a spirit of fear; but a spirit of power, of love and of sound mind."
>
> 2 Tim 1:7

Chapter 2

Reason for Tomorrow

> *If I were asked to give what I consider the single most useful bit of advice for all humanity it would be this: Expect trouble as an inevitable part of life and when it comes, hold your head high, look it squarely in the eye and say, "I will be bigger than you. You cannot defeat me."*
>
> — Ann Landers

I lay awake thinking, today is the last day that I am whole. Tomorrow I would lose a part of me that would not grow back. An obvious part from the heart of me would be missing when the sun goes down.

Not to worry, you'll be fine, said my normally rational mind as I propped myself up in the big bed I shared with my sweet husband. Then a wave of panic passed over me as I realized our marriage story would change tomorrow and I wondered for the one-hundredth time in a week, would I ever lay in bed with a man and feel like a whole woman again.

Stop the thoughts, you have work to do! I yelled at myself. Drag your lazy rear out of this bed and out of this house, before morbid becomes your mood for the day. I wanted to be stern with myself. I needed to be stern with myself in order to go on. I got up out of bed, put on my old comfy sweats and walking shoes, and told myself:

Water the flowers in the semi darkness, feed the cats, and watch for the sunrise. Braless, let them hang where they will and feel the softness as the weighty masses rub against your skin. Walk to the ranch gate and retrieve the newspaper and on the uphill climb, forget that Mother taught you it was taboo to touch yourself in a sensual way.

Lovingly, hold them in your hands and feel their heaviness and languish over the sweat that forms in your palms as you pack them side by side uphill in this humid climate. Run your fingers over the damage already created by the doctor and relish the soreness of the injured breast, for tomorrow you will wish you could feel the hurt spot just one more time.

Too bad you never got to know them other than to tuck them in a bra and occasionally hold them for a hot lover as he blessed them with his lips.

No baby suckled them and it is now hard on your heart to know the decision you made to be childless, because of the hereditary disease you carry, has contributed to form and feed the cancer in your breast. The cancer is the result of not using up what your female body created and then adding more of the same unneeded chemical with the years of birth control pills you swallowed daily.

Only one would be removed and I tried to imagine what it would feel like to be lopsided. Yeah, sure, they could reconstruct it or give you a soft bag of make-believe flesh to tuck in your bra, but how lopsided would you feel in your mind? Although, by listening to all the other dissection stories women had sent my way, it seemed life went on and you learned not to mind at all. *Ha! I bet what they're really trying to tell me is I will cease to mind because I won't allow myself to think of what I have lost. Walk, I told myself. Walk up that hill. Get it over with. Don't look back to see what is following you until you make the turn around at the top. Don't take time to think today. There will be plenty of time for reflection, except my reflection will never be the same. Please, Lord, help me find a way to cope with how my life is changing.*

At the crest of the rocky hill, I stopped at the threshold of the outer world and listened to the beautiful sound of quietness. Strange that the sun had not shown its face in the lateness of this morning. Solid gray were the heavens, reflecting my flat and colorless mood. Many early mornings I had stood there and viewed the valley of the ranch at sunrise: the beauty of the balance of nature. Today, it was hard to make myself turn around and look back the way I came, for in turning, I would be heading full force into what lay ahead. As I made the turn, what would I see?

I found that the two goat-herding dogs had followed me quietly, absorbing my need to be alone. One dog was huge and fluffy and white and her body swayed from side-to-side in a meandering gait as she crested the top of the hill. Her big black nose formed a round node in the middle of downy white. The other was black nosed and sleek with black hair that lay close to her body. Her walk was solid and straight. The two together on the road behind me were as mismatched as my chest would be tomorrow.

On the power lines to my right a pair of doves sat close to each other, facing east as they waited for the morning sun to tell them it was time to fly and start their day. On the top fence wire underneath the pair was a lone dove, sitting quietly without a mate, lacking a partner to share the day. I watched as the first of the sun's rays broke through the gray of the morning. As if on cue, the pair of doves simultaneously raised their wings and took flight, leaving the single dove perched motionless on the fence wire. Would one breast mourn the loss of the other as the dove mourned her missing partner?

Lord, what have I done to deserve this mutilation of my body? Where will I find the strength to do what must be done? I hung my head in shame. I sounded so vain, as if my whole world had always centered on my breasts; a fact that I would not have believed before the doctor's phone call. I forced myself to think of what I hadn't done and tried to minimize the loss of a breast. What I hadn't done was bring a child born with hemophilia into this world to suffer like my brother. What I hadn't done, was punish a small sweet child out of my selfish desire to produce a little person just like me. Instead, I had adopted a beautiful three-day-old baby girl. What I had to do was to give away this fleshy part of my body as payment for my choice to bear or not to bear. I must believe that the cancer had not spread to other parts of my body, even though the telltale lymph nodes had yet to be removed.

I begged my mind to be still and to concentrate on the answer to the "w*hy me*" question I must face tomorrow. *I truly don't think I can manage it, Lord!*

I had one more mind trick left to try. I usually weighed and measured every traumatic incident in my life by asking, "After all, no one died—did they?" and I could *usually* manage to put the event into its proper perspective and go on about my life.

I asked myself the question.

And from somewhere deep within my soul, a forgotten little voice from my childhood answered, "No, but it sure does hurt like they did."

> *My soul is weary with sorrow; strengthen me according to your word.*
> PSALM 119:28

CHAPTER 3

No Place to Cry

Healing is a matter of time, but it is sometimes also a matter of opportunity
                                            HIPPOCRATES

It didn't work. No amount of persuasion from any source could get me to calmly take that ride to the hospital where I would be expected to allow them to slice away my right breast. Pity my sweet husband the hour ride I lay bawling in the back seat, so entirely down on my life. Questioning all that had happened to me in my lifetime: why did he marry me? Why did my brother have to live such a painful life? Why didn't I get that raise I worked so hard for the year before? Why—out of all the kids in my family—did I have to be the one to take my ailing father to the nursing home?

Back and forth my mind raced, to yesterday's worries, problems from thirty years ago, today's dilemma, to Dad's demise two years back. Racing, trying to find a place of comfort but failing miserably and finally spinning out into a wall of blackness in the drug-induced sleep before surgery.

A few hours after the surgery, I awoke and to my greatest surprise, I was still me! I don't know why I thought that losing a breast was going to immediately change me. I had been afraid that when I opened my eyes after the surgery, I would see only gray as if the light of all the joys I had ever received would be gone, vanished, vanquished for ever and ever. I smiled a huge smile and had very little pain. The next morning as I sat combing my long hair, the surgeon came by and said I looked great and he allowed me to go home.

Once at home, I was determined no one would ever see my chest and I wouldn't ask for outside help for the care of the wound. I wanted everyone to back up and let me continue on as if nothing had ever happened and accepted as little help as possible. Food, flowers, and cards flooded the house. Mother, who insisted on staying with me, was in heaven arranging and rearranging the fresh bouquets.

An elderly friend came to give me encouragement to face my tomorrows and she said I turned out to be her inspiration. The grandchildren came and saw that I was still Granny and I again enjoyed playing that role. Life was quickly changing back to good after such depressing weeks before the surgery.

Prompted by so many people genuinely interested in my battle with breast cancer, I decided to write down my experiences. I made a mailing list of women who sent me cards or gifts. With Mother acting as my editor, I began a newsletter. All was well with my world again.

Then, the second week an infection blazed across my chest and threatened to burn through my pajamas and my sweet husband hovered nearby, completely in charge for the first time in our fifteen years of marriage. I had to forgo my promise not to let him see my body as it was now. I had to ask for his help and let him look at my wound. Tears rolled down my face as I watched his eyes take in the alterations of my chest.

Aren't life's rules concerning friendship strange? You can spend fifteen years side-by-side with another person, sharing beds and bathrooms and bills and never be close. But you can hold that same person's hand in the middle of a crowded emergency room or watch your special someone have another hole punched in his arm for yet another IV or blood test and suddenly, just that quick, in a few tiny minutes, in the grasping of that needy hand, you can become fast friends and his every groan becomes your pain too. Eddie and I formed a lifelong friendship that began the minute he looked into my face and said, "Patty, it doesn't look so bad."

Two days in the hospital and six IV bags of antibiotics later, my new friend brought me home wearing, for the first time, a bra with a silky pad tucked in a special slot across my damaged breast. I should have been in heaven, but I cried all the way back to the ranch, remembering over and over again an incident that occurred in the last few hours of my hospital stay.

The morning of my last day in the hospital the cancer clinic sent an angel named Renee to my room bearing a gift bag from the American Cancer Society. It contained books about coping with breast cancer and most importantly, a new bra made especially for patients like me. Slipping it on with her help, I felt completely dressed for the first time in many days! Finally, the lone breast was tucked up in a bra again, and sitting beside it was a soft make-believe pillow that surprisingly matched in size.

I could make myself laugh by thinking about the situations the bra could place me in, as I was instructed to sew something heavy into it on the right side or to hook the soft side to my panties with a garter. Otherwise, the right side of the bra could ride up toward my throat during the day. I laughingly imagined the embarrassment this could cause during a business meeting if I found it floating somewhere just below my chin!

Comfortable with my body for the first time in weeks, I hugged the angel and thanked her profusely and held tightly to her hand when she got up to leave. I was so happy, I cried hard tears believing, in time, I would become comfortable with my chest as it was now and that my mind would soon consider this a minor alteration. I sat in my hospital bed and thanked God for all the help I had been receiving.

Another source of help came from Alice, my roommate in the semi-private room we had shared. She had just had malignant tumors removed from both breasts and was unbelievably alert and mobile, not even taking much pain medicine. Though it was not my habit to share any of my fears or hurts except through my writing, I found it impossible to isolate myself with only the thin curtain pulled between our beds. After the first couple of hours, we became fast friends. As we lay stranded side-by-side on our own semi-private islands of fear that first night, we shared the queasiness of the unknown darkness that lay ahead of us, moored to our surroundings by our individual IV poles, our beds too far apart in the black of the night for us to hold hands.

Privacy in a semi-private room is impossible, and when one of the procedures they used to check for infection hurt or I groaned in the bed while moving about, Alice would ask if I was all right. A young female doctor caught me crying silently in my hospital bed because I was simply worn out from all the worrying and she sat on the side of the bed and prayed out loud for me. When she finished, I heard my neighbor's voice on the other side of curtain telling me she, too, cared for me and that she was also crying for me. I'd never witnessed a sweeter soul than hers.

My sweet roommate outside of this hospital was cool and tough and lively and I gathered, by listening to her, that she was the leader of her household and hadn't the time for setbacks. She had a grown daughter and a retired husband residing in her home, and said she had no place to isolate herself to cry and think about what was happening to her body. My house held the same problem, as I also had no place to cry alone where someone couldn't eventually find me and see my tearstained face.

On the morning we were both due to be dismissed, Alice's husband came early and they sat on the other side of the curtain and were surely forced to listen to my marveling about the new me in my bra, even though I tried to quietly express my joy to the angel bearing the gift. Not wanting Alice's husband to see my new chest before my husband did, I escaped the room, took a book, and went way up the hall to the vacant family waiting room and found a chair in the sun and turned it facing the window. I was determined to stay there until my husband came so I could show him in the privacy of this empty room how normal I could look in the new bra.

Sitting quietly in the warmth of the sun, I assessed my physical and emotional conditions and decided I would be okay! The infection was under control and I was in love again with God and His beautiful world. I was a little weepy from all the medications, but knew they would work out of my system soon and planned on driving to visit friends close to home for a couple of days and build up my stamina and return to work! I was cold, but the sun coming in the window warmed me. I needed to wash my hair but I had washed my body and put on clean pajamas.

I had to admit I was embarrassed about my housecoat, which due to my stupidity in purchasing white, was filthy with red blood spots from an IV line that blew out, orange juice from a breakfast I ate in bed, tan facial makeup from days past, and plain old dirt. On top of all the foreign colors adorning my robe, I had also dug out of the bottom of my makeup bag a yellow-headed diaper pin, which I had clasped through the front seam of my robe about chest high, anticipating opening it slowly as if I were a model, to reveal my new chest to my sweet husband. I looked a little trashy on the outside, but was free of stitches and surgery drains and sad thoughts! I felt as loose as a goose coming in for a soft landing on a blue pond of cool lake water.

In moving slightly to allow my large body to fit between the arms of the waiting-room chair, I noticed the three-day-old brown socks within my sandals. I was a sight after all, but who cared? Happy to be alive, I opened my book.

Lost for a chapter or two, I was brought back to my surroundings by a voice behind me saying, "So, there you are!" and I turned my half-swollen eyes and unmade face toward the female voice, expecting to see a nurse determined to hunt me down for a last blood test before I left the hospital that day. To my total surprise, it wasn't a nurse and who knew why she, of all people, sought me out when my confidence was at such a fragile starting gate to recovery.

Standing not quite five feet tall and weighing at least one hundred pounds less than me was a person I always avoided, even when I looked my best. My old dream of being naked on a stage in front of an audience would not hold a candle to how I felt right then. I was face-to-chest with a perfect form that had clean shiny hair, slim tanned arms, and two real breasts encased in a bright, clean purple blouse. Tears welled up behind my eyelids.

Who was she? Well, in truth, she was a sweet, God-fearing woman and I should have loved her as I did my other sisters in Christ but couldn't force myself. She was my husband's first true love, the woman he fought fights over, the mother of his children, and the person who had shared his first twenty years of adulthood. She was my mother-in-law's constant companion, my two lovely stepdaughters' mom, and four of my sweet grandchildren's' real grandmother. I came into this marriage with great expectations and this little pint-sized lady, standing in front of me, had me beat before my husband even slipped the wedding ring onto my finger.

She was seeing my swollen face, my filthy housecoat, my dirty socks, and worst of all, my new fake chest protruding through the gap clasped together with a yellow-headed diaper pin. She was the first to see what a moment ago I had been so happy to gift wrap in my dirty housecoat and present to my husband as my present to him for all the grief I had put him through those past weeks. *What else could I do?* All my hopes and dreams of a happy next chapter flew away as if leaving the ground on pigeon wings as I realized I was kidding myself about the new me. I was exactly what she saw—a big, dirty, half-breasted, tearstained wreck of a woman sitting pathetically alone in a cold hospital waiting room. Being nice to her between my tears was almost impossible, but I managed by reminding myself she couldn't help it if she were everybody's petite sweetheart.

My biggest fear during her visit was that I expected any minute my husband to round the corner from the elevators and see us highlighted by the morning sun as if we were in a spotlighted scene from an everyday dramatic soap opera. The small pretty woman who broke his heart and the fat, sick woman who wanted more than anything on earth—even the desire to be cancer-free—his whole heart, including and *especially* the jealous part he swore would never surface again after losing his first love.

Time stood still. I desperately wished to be at my ranch gate in the predawn, waiting and listening for the birds in the trees to begin their cacophony of music as the sun rose, for I knew the only music I would be hearing in the next few minutes would be the low chords on a piano, playing *Dum, Dum, Dum,* precluding the disastrous scene soon to be playing right there on Stage 5, or rather Wing 5, of that cancer hospital.

Finally, after what seemed an eternity, she left me alone and I cried from the bottom of my heart, soaking the front of my soiled housecoat and swelling my eyes shut. The joy of a presentable chest was forgotten and the beginning of a new batch of self-confidence was washed away by tears of jealousy and of remorse for feeling that way. By the time my husband arrived I was curled up in my hospital bed, my tear-stained face a sad welcome to his sweet hello.

A few days after that encounter the smile was back on my made-up face and the new bra helped me to feel like my old self but I struggled to understand the visit from the little lady. Was there a point to be made? Did every woman going through Breast Cancer 101 have to come face-to-face at her most vulnerable point with that which she feared the most, whether a first wife or second wife or old rivals at a high school reunion in order for God to reach her? Must we learn to face our devils today and get up the next morning and realize we were still ourselves, nothing lost from the encounter of yesterday but a few tears?

I think Alice was exactly right when she said we had no place to cry where someone couldn't see our tearstained face. For I had to believe that God was always watching over us no matter where we hid and although I sought reasons for why I must cry that day, somewhere at the end of that long cancer walk, the tears would be justified.

My only prayer was that I had enough tears to make it to the end.

Jesus said "Blessed are you who weep now, for you will laugh."

LUKE 6:21

Chapter 4

Journey of Trust

Courage – Fear that has said its prayers.
                        Dorothy Bernard

I felt ready to tackle a full day at my job, back on my feet in less than three weeks since the surgery. I was up way before daybreak and out on the sidewalk in front of our ranch house wrapped in my daughter's favorite old quilt, the quilt her grandmother had made in the shape of a huge brown bear. The night sky was black, the stars were bright, the moon a perfect white circle, almost out of sight around the backside of the sky. The weather had changed from hot and horrible when I left for the hospital to the crispness of an early fall, and I could finally fully focus on the world around me. I stood barefooted on the cool concrete and encouraged myself to breathe slowly and deeply and then a scene from last night invaded my mind, and I had to giggle!

The moon was egg-yolk yellow when it rose in the east last night, and I had come out on this same sidewalk wrapped in this same quilt and stared at it, trying to absorb its light into my body, anticipating recharging my soul with its heavenly glow. The hinges on the old screen door squeaked and I turned to see Eddie coming out into the night, naked, his usual bedtime attire. He was rubbing his eyes and asking me what was I doing and why I wasn't in bed where he had been keeping such a vigilant watch over me for the last weeks.

Explaining that I was hoping to glow like the moon when I came back to bed, he shook his oh-so-manly mind and mumbled something about his not understanding my needing light when most people would be shutting it out and trying to get some sleep. I smiled my "I'm so much more in touch with my soul" smile and offered him protection from the cool wind, and for a few precious seconds, he allowed me to use the bear's arms to hold him captive. We stood pressed together tight, in the dead of the night, under nature's magnificent canopy of light.

Just look at us now, friends to the end! We're sharing not only the everyday "B's" of beds, bathrooms, and bills, but also the moon and the stars and an old brown bear quilt in the middle of the night.

It was so great to share my fears with him and I begged my soul not to let him know how scared I was of what we would have to share next. Now I shook off my panic of tears and remembered last night in the dark, feeling with my bare toes the errant grass somehow growing in the middle of the concrete walk, and of course, like everything else in my life right now, the thought shot through me of the supposed cancer cells running rampant in my body. Invisible cancer was just like that grass that took advantage of the cracked concrete and had run rapidly across the entire width of the sidewalk. I had reasoned in the dark that if I had night vision or even a guiding light, I could see the grass pathway or the cancer's trail across my body and I would know for sure it was there and needed to be destroyed. But, I couldn't see in the dark and luckily I couldn't see or feel the cancer inside my body and had to trust in diplomas and clinical studies and be a guinea pig for scientists without ever positively knowing I even needed to do so! The same question I began asking the first day of my cancer walk rose in me again: *Must I really, Lord?* After all, there had been no cancer evident in the lymph nodes they removed from my body and only the size of the cancerous lump in my breast warranted the chemotherapy treatments.

The security of my life had been shattered like a thin mirror hitting a tiled bathroom floor and today I didn't know if I could even trust the scientists when they said our planet turns and the universe is still. After all, I couldn't feel the ground moving under me! The team of doctors assigned to my case was asking for my confidence but I couldn't cough it up and lay it on a plate and say, "Here it is! Take it, run with it, kill me if you must with your poison, but I'll trust you whole heartily!" After all, I was only a frail and frightened human being and I should not have to make what could turn out to be a totally life-changing or life-ending decision. *Chemotherapy or no chemotherapy?*

Slowly breathing in and out in a calming exercise, I chastised myself, *Quit being silly*, as I knew I must eventually bow to their credentials and leave "How the World Turns" to the experts. Trusting somewhat that I was not just another guinea pig they wished to experiment on by feeding me poisons for the next nine months to see whether or not it really cured the cancer or killed the rest of my organs. Trusting in chemo as a cure was like trusting in a two-sided sword, both sides sharp and sticking in you! No matter which strain of chemotherapy I received, the chemo would kill a part of me, either good or bad or a little of both. The decision had to be made today: did I sign up or take my chances of no treatments? Death or dismemberment, as they would say before a sword fight! *I don't want the chemo, Lord. Help me please with this decision.*

Time for a reality check! I must chuckle now to think my newly found friend would allow me to refuse the treatment. Dream on! He'd put me in the car and deliver me safely again to the hospital and he would put up with ten hours of crying this time just to insure I took the chemo, stating he didn't want to lose me to some future cancer cells. Eddie's stand was firm. He insisted I take every precaution that was offered to completely eradicate any cancer cells.

A phrase came to mind, a little verse I heard a preacher use when someone was on vacation and he wished the congregation to pray for their safe trip and return. He asked for "journey mercies." Lord, give me journey mercies, for I must make this journey and need to have more trust in others than I had ever had in my entire life. Trust must fill up my soul and crowd 'round me as I sat in that first recliner and it must still be there when I sat in the last recliner, taking the poisons a few thousand medical researchers had deemed the best combination for a cancer cocktail. I must trust that when they rolled the dice on which treatment I would receive while participating in the clinical trial, that I received the chemo best suited to kill the cancer cells living inside my body. I must believe that I would come home safely, nine months from today, without cancer and with all my vital organs intact. Safe to wrap up again in the old abandoned bear quilt of my child, standing with my newly found friend under your night sky, trusting that the earth did go 'round and 'round even though I couldn't see it, Lord.

The child's voice inside me began to sing, "Jesus loves me, this I know," and I realized the truth in her words.

> *Trust in the Lord with all your heart and lean not on your own understanding.*
> PROVERBS 3:5

Chapter 5

Bargaining for the Baby

I remember my mother's prayers and they have always followed me. They have clung to me all my life.
— Abraham Lincoln

I persuaded the oncologist to allow me to delay my chemotherapy treatments until my daughter, Sharla, had her baby and her family made their move to an army base in South Carolina. The move was scheduled for when the baby would be a couple of weeks old. I did not want Sharla to concentrate on my illness when she would have her hands full with her first baby and their new surroundings, far, far from home. I felt as if God wanted me to protect Sharla from what was about to happen in my life.

I could block out my fears about taking the chemo by focusing on the new joy that would soon become part of our lives. As they counted down the days until her due date, Sharla and her husband, Michael, insisted that since I had chosen to adopt and had never witnessed a birth, I should be present in the delivery room.

Sharla's labor was long and hard and tiresome and then around 11:00 p.m., the baby started coming. I could see its head crowning and I should have been excited, but what mother could be excited when her daughter seemed in such pain? And then afterward, I wished a thousand times I had not been there as the baby girl came into the world with the umbilical cord wrapped around her neck five times. She was lifeless and limp and the color of gray putty in the doctor's hands. My heart sank into the floor.

The doctor whipped the cord from around her neck and passed her to the nurses, keeping her out of Sharla's sight the entire time. The baby never cried, never moved, never gave any indication that she was alive. I followed the nurses out into the hall but was stopped when they entered another door. I stood with my ear pressed to the door and some twenty minutes later I heard the mewing cry of a newborn baby. *Sharla's or another's?*

What seemed like hours later, they told us the baby was alive but she needed to be transferred to another hospital for neonatal care. We were told to stick close by until an ambulance could arrive to pick up the baby. I went into the darkened waiting room and tried my best to shut my eyes and sleep, but couldn't. God just couldn't allow this to happen to the family; I had to do something!

I went down the hall past the nurse's station and found a woman's restroom with the lights off. By the light of the red exit, I found my way to the center of the room and got down on my knees and pleaded with God to spare the life of Sharla's baby. I tried at first to reason with Him that our family had enough to worry about with my breast-cancer fight and then I tried to make Him feel guilty by asking Him why He needed another baby in heaven when Sharla didn't have even one to hold in her empty arms. Finally, I attempted to bargain:

God, if you will let Sharla's baby live, I will smile every day forward during my battle with breast cancer and I promise I will do whatever you want me to do to help other women diagnosed with breast cancer.

Not knowing anything about the months of treatments or surgeries to come, I reasoned I was offering something that I normally would not have done. I was more prone to frowning than smiling when times got hard and had no idea how to help anyone else with her cancer walk when I had barely started mine.

Feeling better, I felt assured that God agreed to my offer. I got up off my knees and went back down the hall where an ambulance arrived and whisked the little baby and her dad off to another hospital.

Sharla, as always, showed her tough facade as she and I waited for dawn so she could be dismissed sometime during that day and we could follow the baby to her new hospital.

While the two of us were all alone with our thoughts and each other, Sharla turned to me and said, "Momma, the baby is named after you. Her name is Abigail Patricia Williams." I broke down and cried. Sharla held herself together and held me. It had been such a long day for all of us.

Earlier, Eddie had gotten a piece of metal in his eye and part of the time while Sharla was in the labor room, I was downstairs with him in the emergency room. The sliver of steel was removed and he was given a strong sedative to help him overcome the pain. I couldn't leave to drive him home so I called a couple of close friends, Danita and Bobby, and they came and picked him and his truck up from the hospital and deposited him at our ranch. Little did I know that I had made a serious mistake by letting him go home to stay alone.

That morning before Sharla could be released from the hospital, I drove to the ranch to clean up a little and check on Eddie. I found him completely out of his mind from the sedative and contemplating hanging himself in the barn! The combination of the worry about my breast cancer and the serious condition of Sharla's baby at birth, plus, a sedative way too strong for his system, had rendered him completely hysterical. I called the pharmacy and they advised me to flush the rest of the medicine down the toilet and never give it to him again. Another set of friends came to the house and sat with him.

I was too tired to maneuver in the Austin traffic and Sharla and I rode with my niece, Debbie, to see Sharla's little Abby in the neonatal wing of an Austin hospital. Claiming my rights as a grandmother, I was allowed to see Abby later on in the day. My first thought was to thank the Lord that she was now a healthy pink color. The tubes and wires attached to her body and the doctor's dire predictions of the medical and mental problems she could experience if she survived the next few days, scared us all to death.

Poor Sharla. Not only was her baby's life in jeopardy, she had no place to stretch out during the daylight hours between visits to the neo-natal wing. Even though she was still swollen and uncomfortable from giving birth, she refused to go home. Luckily, the *Ronald McDonald House* had a room available for Sharla and Michael and they stayed in Austin near their new baby. I returned to the ranch late that night after having checked on Eddie by telephone several times during that day.

It seemed nothing could go right for our family and I was depressed and worried the baby would not make it or that she would have serious health problems if she did. I walked through the house and heard Eddie snoring quietly in the bedroom and decided I needed to let off a little pent-up steam. I went out in the backyard and picked up two pecan branches that had blown down in a recent windstorm and went out on the front sidewalk in the complete darkness and beat those two sticks together until my arms ached. I told the Devil several times during my beating frenzy to get away from our house and leave us alone! When I finally went to bed, it occurred to me that town folk probably never got to express their true feelings and that I should feel lucky to live on the ranch. I gave God a smile and a thank you and He blessed me with a restful sleep.

The next day, Eddie was himself again and little Abby was still alive!

> *You will call, and the Lord will answer: you will cry*
> *for help and He will say: Here I am.*
> ISAIAH 58:9

Chapter 6

Close, but Not the Purring Stage

Be so true to thyself, as thou be not false to others.
FRANCIS BACON

The loud buzz announced someone sought entrance into the neo-natal unit where Abigail slept quietly in her incubator. Glancing up at the picture on the monitor captured by the camera outside the door, Sharla and I saw Rissa, one of my stepdaughters. Leaving our watchful post, we exited the sterile unit and greeted her, and Eddie's mother, Alice Beth. Looking past their shoulders I saw a third figure. Eddie's ex-wife was standing quietly behind them. My look of dismay at seeing her was apparently obvious, as she turned her face away and stared at the ground a few seconds before stepping forward and inquiring about the baby.

Without consciously thinking about it, I assessed myself as I assumed she was assessing me. Had I remembered to dress that morning? What did I have on? How fat did I look? I hadn't taken time to wash my hair again for the second day in a row, did it look dirty?

While I counted off my apparent flaws, Sharla explained Abigail's medical condition. All her organs, except for her heart, took great blows from oxygen deprivation during birth. Thankfully, each day had shown an improvement in their functions. Another main concern was her low white-blood count. A blood transfusion might be required.

If she continued to improve and was released, time could reveal other problems. The doctors had recited a list of things that could be wrong. She might be moderately to severely mentally retarded or even worse, she might be a vegetable.

Scrubbing again, Sharla went back inside and opened a blind covering a window near Abigail's bed. I stood back and watched the ladies ooh and awe at my granddaughter. If you ignored the tubes and the wires attached to her body, she was a very beautiful, seven pound baby, with a shock of thick dark hair. My heart swelled with pride. Love for little Abby kept me focused on what was important.

Agreeing she was beautiful, the ladies promised to keep her in their prayers. I walked them to the elevator and stood talking for a few minutes about how hard it had been on Sharla to get up out of bed within six hours of delivery. Her legs and feet were still terribly swollen and she had only allowed herself a few hours of rest at their room at the Ronald McDonald House. Michael was driving daily the hour long trip back and forth from base, trying to tie up loose ends for their impending move. He had to report to Drill Instructor School at an Army base in South Carolina in ten days. It was doubtful that Sharla and the baby would be able to accompany him.

It all sounded impossible. How could Michael go off and leave them knowing he might not see his baby again? Unbidden, the rest of my worries came tumbling out. How would I cope if they were all able to leave? Sharla and I had never been more than a couple of hours away from each other. Their departure would also trigger my start of chemo infusions. Tears began to run down my checks. I berated myself! What was I doing? I didn't intend to show my weaknesses in front of Eddie's first love!

The elevator door opened and a smiling group of people emerged and headed in the direction of the well-baby unit. Looking down at the floor so they could not see my tearstained face, I felt arms around me. Arms foreign in their touch. I realized they were the same arms that had hugged my husband and brought him comfort for twenty years. I didn't struggle. I stood still and felt their warmth. My thoughts were of a stray cat that took weeks to tame. Finally, if you tried long enough, and didn't lose your patience, the cat would let you hold her captive. She might shake in your grasp, but eventually, if you accepted her fears as yours, a trust formed.

As the three ladies stepped onto the elevator, I lifted my gaze and looked at her face. I didn't see any signs that she was judging me, no pity, and no disapproving shake of her head. As the elevator door closed, a spark of doubt ignited a corner of the ugliness I kept piled like fallen leaves in my mind. Could it be that I was the one holding court? Perhaps it was time I took a good long look in the mirror. I had a feeling I wouldn't like the person peering back at me.

In the silence of that same night when sleep escaped me, my mind replayed the hug I'd received at the neo-natal unit. I had been caught off guard by her show of compassion. True, I wasn't at the "purring stage" but definitely her patience had paid off. Would I be more comfortable around her the next time our paths met? Would horns of jealousy sprout once again? Or, did sweet babies have a way of melting needless fences as easily as a warm liquid poured on a lump of sugar?

Concentrating on Abby's sweet face, I almost drifted off to sleep. Then I thought about the last thing the doctor's had told Michael and Sharla about Abigail. A test they ran showed the baby was deaf. Little Abby wasn't going to be able to hear the world going on around her. Somehow I felt as if I had caused her problems at birth although I knew I was being silly. Oh, Lord, I ask for your forgiveness of my many sins. Please don't let my Abigail be deaf because of my transgressions. I'll act better tomorrow, I promise.

With tears streaking down my face, I finally went to sleep. Again, God gave me peaceful sleep in which I dreamed of a field of yellow wildflowers beside our ranch house with bordering trees full of noisy birds. Sitting in Aunt Lucinda's old porch swing, similar to the one hanging on my patio, I rocked a toddler who grinned each time a Mockingbird gave his rendition of a Blue Jay's call. The toddler looked a lot like Sharla at that age. Only time would tell if my dream would come true.

> *Every good and perfect gift is from above, coming down from the Father of the heavenly lights, who does not change like shifting shadows.*
>
> JAMES 1:17

Chapter 7

Seeking Cinderella

Do you love me because I am beautiful, or am I beautiful because you love me?
    OSCAR HAMMERSTEIN II, CINDERELLA

I arose from bed and gathered my shampoo and conditioner and leaned my long hair over into the kitchen sink and felt the coolness of the stainless steel under my elbows. My custom of washing my hair each morning in the sink was difficult now as it was hard to get the right angle to lay the right side of my chest on the cabinet. The piece left for reconstruction of my breast was long and hard and it wrapped from the front of my chest around to the back side of my underarm. It was strange to feel it pouching out as it did from beneath my pajamas as if a foot-long hot dog was suspended from my upper body. I was determined to find a comfortable spot for this hot dog to lie as I wanted to enjoy this last washing of my long hair.

My hair, or upcoming loss of it, became a great focal point to take my mind off the imminent departure of Sharla and her baby. Michael had already reported to the base in South Carolina and his mother had arrived to help Sharla pack and make the long drive. Abigail had spent ten days in the hospital and appeared to be healthy enough to make the move but she cried often. Just the thought of them halfway across the United States, put me in tears. Not only would I be concerned about their welfare, Sharla would be worried about me. I needed a distraction.

I would have nearly a foot of long auburn hair cut off by a beautician and sent to an organization that makes wigs for children who have lost their hair due to adverse medical conditions or treatments. Hopefully, I would be able to discard my growing concern of losing my femininity by picturing my hair blowing in the wind while perched on a child's head. I had discovered that I could occupy my mind and forget about the fear of the chemo treatments by focusing on the months I would spend baldheaded. Also, thinking about my hair starting to fall out twelve or thirteen days after the first chemotherapy treatment kept me from worrying about the first chemotherapy treatment itself.

If you saw me fully dressed after the right breast was removed, you couldn't tell I had ever had any surgery, but, when I became baldheaded everyone would know I was sick. How would I cope with all the sympathy? I tried my best to brush these worries from my mind as I sat on the back porch and ran my old purple comb thru my long hair before I washed it for the last time.

Wash it, rinse it, comb it. Feel the heaviness of your wet hair on your shoulders. Experience the feel of the water rivulets running down your face and neck and soaking into your pajamas. Push open the glass door to the porch and stumble over fat cats who lie close to the crack under the door, seeking the sliver of air conditioning as it escapes to cool their fur-lined bodies.

As I combed my hair and let the strong south wind blow it dry, a thought played across my mind and I wanted, just that once, to drop kick the cats' lazy bodies clear across the yard! I was envious of their fur shining in the morning light. Jealousy and anger had consumed my emotions all night. My mind had replayed a couple of scenes from long ago when I had walked up on Eddie while he was inspecting another woman as she passed by. I kept asking over and over again, *if he didn't find me attractive back then, what did he feel now?* When the baldness of my head glistened like a glass Christmas-tree ornament in the nightlight of our room, what would he think of me? When my hair was removed, following close behind the loss of my breast, he would no longer find me desirable or the least bit attractive. I hung my head in shame, thinking about how much of my femininity I lost undergoing a complete hysterectomy a few years back.

Lord, you know, I was really counting on giving up only the breast, not my hair too! I will be so naked without it gathered around my shoulders. Why do I have to give up my hair? I fear I am losing everything that makes me a woman.

Why did the doctor have to prescribe chemo? I had a terrible time sitting in that little examination room listening to the doctor say, "Let's be on the safe side and go ahead and make sure the cancer is gone," and then having to listen to her recite the possible adverse side effects of the chemo infusions. Chemotherapy was definitely poison when they put it in you and poison when you peed it out.

Are we setting me up for a future on this earth, Lord, or will I be quickly joining you in heaven? If it's heaven where I'm heading soon, let's skip this chemo and let me keep my hair!

I doubted at my age that I would ever grow my hair out long again and I wanted a record of its existence to frame and place on my husband's dresser so he would be able to remember what I looked like before. I had scheduled a sitting to have my picture made that morning before my afternoon appointment to cut off my hair. It was important to remove my healthy hair before the first chemo ran through my veins in just a few short days, as it would turn my beautiful hair into dry, brittle strands.

I would add a third task to my agenda for this day. After my hair appointment, I would go to the wig shop and try on different styles and colors of wigs. I would complete all three tasks completely alone. I wanted no one to witness my backward metamorphosing. Instead of emerging as a colorful butterfly after Mother Nature worked her magic for days on end, in only four short hours, I would turn into a dull worm.

By drawing on all my inner strength and repeating the verse, "*I can do everything through Christ who gives me strength*" Philippians 4:13, I made it through the day. During the photography session, I had to fiercely concentrate on anything other than why I was having my picture made, as I did not want the camera to capture any sign of fear in my eyes. To my surprise, my hair appointment was not that traumatic, after my hair was washed, rinsed, and dried, the beautician cut it off just above the large rubber band she had placed around it. As she placed my thick pony tail in a paper sack, I envisioned a little girl wearing two thick braids made from my hair.

But, when the wig specialist put a tight skull cap on my head to give me the illusion of baldness while she slowly searched through her gallery for the perfect wig, I took one look in the mirror and lost all of the composure I had worked so hard to keep during the day. A fifty-year-old bald-headed and very round-faced woman sat staring back at me. The butterfly had definitely lost her vibrancy.

No one could have softened this experience for me even if I had allowed them to hold my hand and tell me it would be all right. Now I understood how I would look and feel about myself when baldness arrived in a few short weeks. By the time the wig specialist returned, I had lost my beauty and my dignity and barely regained my composure when she placed the first wig on my head. For the next hour, she did her best to make me forget about the inevitable loss of my hair and she concentrated fully on making the colorful butterfly reappear.

I remembered a story from childhood, no matter how Cinderella was dressed—whether in ashes or gowns complimented by a pair of beautiful glass slippers—it was her inner beauty that shone for the entire world to see. What she wore only enhanced it. I prayed hard that my inner beauty would overcome my outward appearance and that the "Cinderella" in me would shine through.

The family never knew how hard it was for me to bury my anger over the loss of my breast and then my hair, but one poor stranger certainly did. I kept all my emotions bottled up inside until one day when I had a heart-to-heart conversation with a salesman who called the third time in a week asking for my husband. I quietly told him that I didn't think my husband would be interested in his wares because I was bald and possibly dying of cancer. *Couldn't he wait and call back after I was gone?*

The poor salesman never called our house again and I worry sometimes that I may have ruined his career. At least, I told myself, your sense of humor is returning!

*Consider how the lilies grow. They do not labor
or spin. Yet I tell you, not even Solomon in all his
splendor was dressed like one of these.*

LUKE 12:27

Chapter 8

Okay! I Got It!

Change your thoughts and change your world.
NORMAN VINCENT PEALE

I stood in the drive-way, waving goodbye at my daughter and her baby girl headed for South Carolina, doing a pretty fair job of not crying. My left arm was strapped across my chest to keep it immobile as a port for the chemo infusions had been embedded just above my elbow. I was mad at myself for not making the surgeon wait until Sharla left as I had not been able to properly hold Abby since they had insisted on installing the round metal object just under the skin. Now, I couldn't hug her or Sharla. They were gone!

Eddie, never one for good-byes or scenes that might involve crying women, vacated the ranch earlier, having given Sharla hugs along with safety tips for women traveling alone on the interstates. Mike's mother, Kittie, who had flown down from her home in Tennessee, was in the driver's seat, ready to do her part in helping the children make their long move. What little bit I had been around her led me to believe Sharla had married into a family similar to ours where the women took charge when the going got rough. Mother-in-law problems would never be a topic of conversation Sharla would need to join.

Letting all my tears flow since the car had disappeared through the last of the ranch's gates, I cried loudly. How could all this be happening at one time? Abby sick and barely out of the hospital, Sharla moving to South Carolina, me, fixing to take chemotherapy! It wasn't fair! Crying my heart out, I started toward the house and saw my van sitting patiently in the garage, waiting for me to get behind the wheel and take off to wherever I so desired.

"Straighten up! What are you crying about now? You're getting to be the biggest bawl baby I've ever seen. You cry about this, you cry about that. Stop it, right now!" Patty Cakes was talking, imitating Tommy, my oldest brother. Her high-pitched voice demanding I straighten up.

I let myself into my car and sat in the soft seat. Reaching for a tissue out of the box I kept handy for my now-days way too often crying jags, I wiped my eyes and blew my nose. Patty Cakes, sans Tommy, was right. Nothing stood in my way of following Sharla right now. I could pack a bag and leave within the hour. I could drive one-handed across the whole United States if I wanted to. Nothing was keeping me here but common-sense and chemotherapy. My child was not gone for good, just out of sight.

"Oh, no! Don't start crying again," warned Patty Cakes. "What's the matter with you this time?"

This time, I was crying for two other mothers: mother's that had lost their children, both in automobile accidents. I had been at the funeral for Brian, Billie Jean's son, and had been in awe at the way in which she had handled herself. Broken-hearted as she was over her loss, her faith showed through. Walking as a group the few blocks from the Methodist Church to the cemetery for the burial had been surreal. The air was heavy and a huge white cloud loomed over us as if God's shadow was hovering right above our heads. That night, a powerful storm lashed out with frightening lightning and extremely hard rains as if God, too, was mad that Billie Jean had lost her son before his scheduled time of departure.

Alice Beth, Eddie's mother, had lost her only daughter, Lisa, on

Senior Day. It seemed the communities in our area were notorious for suffering the loss of a graduating senior each year. That particular year, Alice Beth's daughter went to heaven and left a grieving family behind.

Eddie had been married to his first wife at the time and she had vowed to make up for the loss. Knowing how much I hurt, right then, with Sharla gone but really only out-of-sight, I began to understand how badly Alice Beth had needed someone. Alice Beth had allowed her to fill a huge void in her life when Lisa had died so tragically. Did it take my losing Sharla to the military life for me to get the picture? Is that what this is all about, Lord, my experiencing the same sort of hurt so you could make your point?

Okay! I got it! My heart aches, and it must be only a smidgeon of what mother's feel when their children are taken to heaven before them. Forgive me, Lord.

Patty Cakes was quiet. She had disappeared down deep into a corner ready to resurface the next time I seemed out of control. Was it possible that she, the child, and I, the adult, had changed places?

One of the few Bible verses I had memorized years ago came to mind. Did Eddie's ex-wife repeat it to Alice Beth when Lisa died? If so, how dare I take offense to something so beautifully declared!

> *Where you go I will go, and where you stay, I will stay. Your people will be my people and your God my God. Where you die I will die, and there I will be buried. May the Lord deal with me, be it ever so severely, if anything but death separates you and me.*
> RUTH 1:16, 17

Chapter 9

Snip, Snip

It always comes down to the same necessity; go deep enough and there is a bedrock of truth, however hard.
—Mary Sarton

Shortly after I learned to ride a bicycle, I decided life was too hard at home and planned an escape on the paved road that paralleled the railroad track by our house. This road must lead to some faraway and much better place. As this was in the 1950s and we were quite poor and we had no suitcases or spare paper sacks that Momma wouldn't need for trash or treasure storage, my packing must be light. After careful consideration about what I would need to run away from home, I resorted to tying one clean pair of panties to my old rusted bicycle basket.

Being that I could pedal pretty fast and my knots were always loose, the panties only lasted two blocks before they blew out and landed halfway up in a rose bush in a strange neighbor's yard. Getting them down was a joint effort between me and their bulldog and my hands and my underwear were pretty sliced up from the thorns and the dog's super hold on the elastic edge. Of course, Momma, after I got home with shredded hands and underwear and because she did not quite understand what brought on the whole "leaving home" episode, left a mark or two on the very bottom I was trying so hard to ensure would be clean for another day of biking.

At first I thought the lesson from my early days was not to run away from home until you were old enough to figure out how to protect your clean underwear. But, over the years I decided that even a planned escape from any of my life settings would end up only two blocks from my beginning. I learned to stay and grin and bear it until God moved me on. I was always reminded when the urge to run overshadowed my shaky stand-and-fight attitude, of the determination of the bulldog and the strength of the rose bush as they fought me for my underwear.

These last few months facing the cancer and the chemo and now the new baldness and coldness of my body had me at that "runaway stage" several times. I think longingly of a warm beach and me, with a full head of hair and a two-breasted body, absorbing the sunshine by day. I also guiltily dreamed of a warm body at night to wrap up around me and keep me warm. My protector in the living room watching football was wonderful, but his timidness in not wanting to hurt any of my wounds or give me a virus he carried by staying away from me and building what he considered a safe wall around me, left me lonely. I secretly yearned for arms and legs that lacked the knowledge of my cancer that would wrap their long limbs around me and make me warm again. *Surely Lord, I am not the only cancer patient who feels so isolated.*

Today, I decided to try and set aside my feeling of isolation and give in to my lately overpowering need to "cut" something. I would trim the houseplants. Why, after my hair started falling out in mass, my head shearing wasn't so bad! It even got pretty comical when my sister, Stella, shaved a big X on the top of my head and threatened to leave it there to repay me for all the crazy things I had done to her over the past fifty years. So, this morning I thought come on, let's have some fun and see if you can get constructive with your own pair of kitchen scissors! I got started right away on a little ivy trimming. What was good for some of us should be good for all.

Now, you have to consider that some of my ivies have been growing in the same location for at least six years and had six or seven easy feet of runners. I snipped a little here and snipped a little there and the floor of the utility room became as cluttered as the tile floor my own shaved hair rested on after being snipped from my head. About thirty minutes into the trimming of a dozen plants, my sweet husband came through the house searching for where I had "gone off to." Needless to say, he tarried but just a moment and asked no questions as sharp scissors in the hands of a cold and confused "slightly off-her-feed woman" tends to stop all arguing in our house about just who's in charge on such a special day.

Once I wrenched the scissors away from my right hand and hauled off the two enormous trash bags of cuttings, my houseplants had definitely taken on the new hairstyle of their owner. Not exactly a work of art but a new look emerged. Would the plants be cold tonight? Somewhere in the back of my mind I felt a little bad about my need to snip. Okay, I'd let them share my fantasy. Tonight when I lay in bed and dreamed of my beach, my perfect head of thick hair, my sculpted two-breasted body, and the long limbs of a stranger wrapped around me holding me tight, I would set the scene inside a beautiful green shelter made completely of long entwined ivy.

Hmm, this scene was so inviting I wanted to hunt up my old rusty bicycle, securely tie a clean pair of panties to the basket, set out again on that paved road by our old house, and go back to the exact time I heard the dog running beside me, seconds before my panties blew through the air into the rose bush. I almost made it to my imagined place of comfort and would desperately like to try again. Oh, to be there instead of here with a green flannel blanket pulled over my head, waiting for my hair to grow back! I pray for patience, Lord.

> *Come to me, all you who are weary and burdened*
> *and I will give you rest.*
> MATTHEW 11:28

Chapter 10

Tunnels in Time: The Ant Lion

You can't be brave if you've only had wonderful things happen to you.
— Mary Tyler Moore

My lack of hair caused me to have many dreams of Patty Cakes and her head of long golden curls. When I was young, my sister was in charge of combing my hair and we had a battle of our own as she tried to coax out the tangles. Along with the dreams, other forgotten and long-buried memories surfaced also.

Sunlight was always slanted in these dreams, surely in remembrance of the time spent held against my will by my kidnapper in the backseat of an old black Chevrolet when I was four years old. Quietly peering through my tears into the face of the odd man, I watched thousands of dust particles floating lazily from the car's cloth headliner. Dust was framed by the sunlight streaming between the boards of the old car-shed as it slowly settled on his shoulders.

I blinked back the paste created from the dust and my tears and quickly wished I hadn't because I could see him more clearly. Everything about him seemed brown—his clothes, his hair, his creepy eyes, and his brown coffee breath. I closed my eyes and wished to disappear like in a magic trick. It didn't happen so I tried again, but to no avail. I remembered the magical way my sister had held her breath last week when she had retrieved Momma's scissors from the bottom of the swimming hole. My brothers said that when my sister was underwater and holding her breath, she became like a fish and could have swum away and lived forever in the deepest of the dark water.

I was so glad when her face broke the surface of the water and she returned to us as my big sister that I hadn't taken the time to consider the possibilities of holding your breath and escaping from scary places. I could see now how this could help. I puffed out my cheeks and held my breath, concentrating on making a fish face, and although I pressed my lips tightly together and gave it my all, I succeeded in holding my breath for only a minute. Instead of disappearing from the car, I expelled moisture onto our faces as my breath escaped in one long release of air.

The man's wide face registered puzzlement as he lifted his hand to wipe the wetness from his face and then mine. I tried to push the back of my head further down into the seat, but was stopped by my head's soreness. I had forgotten he had wrapped his hands in my long blonde hair and used it to lift me over the short picket fence separating our back yards.

His hand stopped short of my face and hung there in mid-air. Suddenly the musty smell of the inside of that old Chevy that had been parked for years in the same car shed overpowered my short attention span. I forgot about fish faces as a way to escape and lay there perfectly still while a lifelong memory began to form, a frantic memory, which was easily brought to the surface each time I entered the old hardware store in our small town. I called it the dusty smell of stagnant time. Time stood perfectly still as I waited for his next move.

Slowly, some of his fingers spread my long blonde curls across the scratchy brown fabric of the seat, momentarily sticking the strands to the upholstery alongside of my head. I was terrified as he hadn't spoken a word since he had captured me and put me in his car, and this added to his strangeness. For sure, Momma would have told me to avoid this odd man. This thought of Momma made me start to cry silently for her and I wanted to yell, *"Where are you, Momma?"*

Looking desperately for her face, I searched outside the car window behind his head, but all I saw were weathered boards nailed together to form the car-shed door. I remembered hearing him pull the big half door across the sandy floor when I was tucked up under his arm and I thought sadly of all the ant-lion traps and tunnels he had ruined dragging the heavy door across their dirt town. I had played with those same ant lions yesterday before Momma caught me in his yard. Now they were gone, ruined by this quiet man in his haste to hide me in his shed.

His hand started to move again toward me and panic rose in my little chest and threatened to smother me. My already very creative and now terrified little mind took over. Suddenly, I was no longer Patty Cakes, but was instead an ant lion hiding in the bottom of a perfectly formed ant trap, with a dirt tunnel right beside me ready for my escape. I started to burrow my way deep into the sand, finally getting away from this terrifying situation and I was so excited!

As his hand straightened the pink ribbon sewn to the front of my dress, I struggled ten times harder to concentrate on being the ant lion. I closed my eyes tighter and dug deeper into my make-believe tunnel, trying not to choke on the dust I was stirring up with my digging. My intention was to dig further and further away from him, but I could manage it only if I continued to be the ant lion.

The tunnel was getting darker. There was no place to go when I got tired of digging. *What would become of me then?* Another fear popped into my mind, my brothers had cautioned me about digging too deep with my big spoon in the sandy back yard because I would dig up the Devil's big toe. How deep was too deep? I imagined a big dirty toe wiggling in front of me right now and I struggled to find a turn in the tunnel that would carry me away.

Doggone my brothers! So many times they had teased about what a baby I was and soon I would tire and prove them right and I'd be trapped somewhere beneath the car-shed in a dark dusty tunnel. I couldn't hold my breath for very long. *How would I escape?* My little heart was beating harder and faster and the dirt was starting to pile up closer to my body, leaving me very little room to dig.

Then I saw it! Directly in front of me was a wooden door. Where had I seen it before? I struggled in this dark place to clean off the little window mounted in the wood, trying to let in enough light to recognize the door. Finally when I thought my mind would run out of possibilities before I came up with the right answer, I heard someone knocking loudly. I saw that door every day! I must be standing on the other side of the door where Jesus was knocking in the picture that hung on my bedroom wall. On my bedroom wall inside my very own house!

Momma said Jesus was knocking and waiting for someone to let Him into their heart and I already did this at Sunday school, didn't Jesus remember? *Let me out, Jesus!* I wanted to go home! I saw His face clearer now and Jesus' eyes looked so kind that I started to whimper and feared I would lose my concentration on the only escape door available out of this very real nightmare.

Just as a watery sob threatened to drown me inside my dirt tunnel, I heard for the first time in my life the noise that assured me even today that I am not abandoned in a long dark tunnel, a sound that has followed me through time; a saving sound. No, it wasn't a bell or a voice or a siren. It was simply the rattling of a door handle, a jostling sound, the steady sound of some unseen hand turning the knob back and forth seeking entrance. *Jesus opened the wooden door and let me out!*

The car door was opened by a big-bellied man wearing a shiny badge and when he held me tightly and tried to assure me that I would be all right, I couldn't help but notice that his breathe smelled exactly like the scary man's. I quickly turned my face away from his and cried for Momma. In just a few short minutes, I was placed once again in the comforting arms of my mother and she held me until my trembling subsided.

Later on, in our living room, the sheriff asked me questions in a little singsong voice, insulting me, the courageous ant lion, with his baby talk. I answered only the questions he asked, offering nothing about the tunnel and my encounter with Jesus at the wooden door. The adults agreed I appeared unharmed and the house filled with more family and neighbors and became much too noisy after I had spent so much time earlier in the quiet tunnel.

For once, my brothers couldn't think of anything to tease me about. They gathered with other men around the car shed next door where they stood and debated the fate of a man, who from birth was never quite right in his head. I grew tired of all the commotion and the attention and crawled up beside my sister on the double bed we shared and stared at the picture of Jesus on the bedroom wall with my little pair of tired green eyes. Eyes that weren't quite as innocent as they were earlier that morning.

I smiled up at Jesus and remembered that I had a secret! A secret I would manage to keep only until the next time I was at Sunday school where I would inform my teachers that I knew, for a fact, that Jesus did not drink coffee. Of course, after my proclamation circulated throughout the entire Methodist Church, my brothers had yet another reason to tease me, but no matter how hard they tried, neither of them ever made me reveal how I knew this to be true.

Finally my eyes grew heavy and I allowed myself to drift off to sleep, not knowing there would come another time in my life when I would feel kidnapped and need to don the persona of the ant lion to get through another imaginary tunnel. Luckily, again this time, the tunnel did not close in around me nor did I lose my concentration on the wooden escape door. For I have learned what makes its handle rattle; prayers sent to heaven for my safety from the many people who love me.

Whether you turn to the right or to the left, your ears will hear a voice behind you saying, "This is the way; walk in it."

ISAIAH 30:21

Chapter 11

Armor of the Arbor

Backward, turn backward, O Time, in your flight.
Make me a child again just for tonight!
        ELIZABETH AKERS ALLEN 1832-1911

I wore a mask when I went to church to protect myself from other people's germs. If feeling really brave, I removed the mask when singing and took a chance that someone behind me might send his flu virus into my air space. It was hard to believe that I was so vulnerable even in the house of our Lord, but not a safe place existed to hide out while your white-cell count was so low. True safe places in life are hard to find. Yet, I remembered how protected I felt as a child, under the old brush arbor when we met for revivals. I wanted to be little Patty Cakes again.

The old brush arbor stood silently awaiting revival time each year. Leafless branches from last-year's cuttings, tied across the post supports, allowed an expansive view of winter's gray sky as the arbor waited patiently for its yearly adornment of fresh and green-leafed willow branches. Field mice, in search of food, and an old tomcat in search of field mice, lost sight of each other in the tall weeds growing near the arbor's outskirts. A few patches of thirsty rescue grass and a circular mound of big red ants wrongly assumed this abandoned dirt floor under the shade of the arbor was theirs to keep and each increased their territory a little more every day. A stray milk cow, stopping by to graze on her way to greener pastures, left a "meadow muffin" as her calling card, where work boots and shiny Sunday shoes had mingled during last summer's revival.

One bright, hot, summer day, during the pause between seeding and harvesting, a handful of farmers and ranchers representing several denominations arrived with their pickups loaded down with willow branches. They used skills that equaled those of Grandma Flossie as she deftly laid the lattice work atop one of her treasured apple pies. They weaved a covering to shade the heads of the soon-to-be assembled group of worshipers. The clumps of grass under the arbor would shortly learn just whose dirt they were growing in, as field hoes in the hands of the farmers quickly uprooted them and raked the area clean. A little kerosene poured into the opening in the center of the ant mound would settle the land dispute for awhile. The whack of hammers pounding nails into board planking echoed off the nearby rock buildings as the workers crafted makeshift tables for the revival's ending meal. The closest outhouse, which could proudly seat two sinners in their need of some relief, would be dusted free of the clingy, springy multiples of granddaddy longlegs, cleared of any wasps and yellow-jacket nests, and the holes freshly limed.

The first night of the revival, a piano wrapped loosely in a wagon sheet would arrive in the back of a farm truck with bright red dirt clinging to its rollers. The men who had the arduous task of rolling it out of the church, into the back of the truck, and out again at the brush arbor were wet with sweat from all the pushing and pulling before the service could start. They would greatly welcome a drink from one of the cold jars of water brought from home, glass jars with screw-on lids, wrapped in pieces of burlap tow sack to keep them cool. The surrounding small country churches brought both their members and their long wooden pews to join in the revival, pews that were well worn from countless bottoms and nicked in several places from their annual trek to the brush arbor, a ride in which half of their length protruded over the pickup's tailgate with children riding happily on the cab end to keep the pews balanced in the truck bed.

Songbooks were used at every service and the books arrived at the arbor stacked haphazardly on empty feed sacks between the piano and the sideboards of the truck. Being careful not to dislodge too many of the grass burrs and sharp goatheads that clung to the burlap sacks, we kids were quick to grab a stack of books and pass them out to the gathering congregation. We knew from years past that our nightly work of distributing and collecting the songbooks would earn us each a nickel when the revival ended.

Probably the nickel was given to us in hopes that we would surrender it to a future collection plate, but we had other plans for our hard-earned money. A nickel would buy a tube of red-skinned peanuts and a grape or orange *Nehi* at the old store just across the road from the brush arbor. It didn't matter that we wouldn't get our nickel until the songbooks were loaded back into the pickup for the last time, or that the store was closed during the revival services at night, because the anticipation of the visit to the store was almost as good as actually holding the cold bottle and tasting the salty peanuts. Many a small tussle broke out among us youngsters as we pushed and shoved in a very un-Christian like attitude to retrieve a stack of books and guarantee our nickel reward.

Distant family members, who only gathered at revival time each year, sympathized with the bereaved that had lost loved ones and admired the newest generation born in the last twelve months, taking the time to remind each other that God never shut a door that He didn't open a window. Ladies came armed with flowered fans from home, or used the cardboard ones on which the local funeral home advertised, to coax a breeze around their faces and keep the gnats away from their sleeping children. Babies were hushed during the preaching with a "sugar tit" made from a lump or two of sugar and tied into a handkerchief, or sometimes if their momma had it available, a tiny chunk of honeycomb was placed in the handkerchief and offered to the baby instead. Insects baited by the glow of the lanterns buzzed around the faces of the contented babies in hopes of stealing a taste or two from a baby's sticky cheeks and their mothers' fan would become a weapon, as she used it to dash away a wasp or bee flying too close to her precious infant.

The singing could be heard for half a mile. No amplifiers or speakers needed to boost the voice of a spirit-filled revival. My grandfather, the song leader, took requests from the congregation and we sang every verse of the chosen hymns, with special enthusiasm on a chorus where one set of singers held onto a word, while the others repeated what was just said. When the singing was over that night and until time came around for altar call and for us to stand as the obligatory offering was collected for the preacher, the youngest of the children were allowed to amuse themselves by playing with the ant lions, or "doodle bugs" awaiting their prey in little cone-shaped pits the insect had dug in the freshly raked dirt under our feet.

At first, I watched the congregation to see who squirmed when the preacher spoke of the abomination of sin stored in each one of us sinners. Then I would try my best to figure how many sins were out there in the world and who might sin the most in our community. I struggled with the question of when, in the midst of all the farming and cooking and churchgoing and sleeping, did people have time to do all this sinning? Did Methodist's sin mostly in the morning and the Baptists mostly in the afternoon? Did men, or maybe children, sin more than the others did? And what the heck was an abomination anyway; and did I have an enlarged one, similar to my swollen tonsils that might need to be removed one day?

Most mommas would forget about you if the preacher was doing his job and when I got tired of meditating on "religious" questions, I sometimes could get all the way underneath the pew and count how many pieces of gum were stuck there and maybe have time to destroy a dirt dauber's nest or two before she caught me. Many times, after I had been threatened and dusted off enough to suit my momma, I would be persuaded to settle down and would lie in my mother's arms and stare up into her sweet face and drift off into a devil's free sleep. Surely I was well protected as long as the loud-talking preacher kept on "shooing" Satan away from his little family of God. On each of these nights, the arbor became my armor, protecting me from all the scary things lurking just outside the glow of light cast by the few Coleman lanterns.

I remember wondering on nights before the humid air, the safety of my mother's lap, and the preacher's tirade against the Devil allowed me to sleep, if maybe the preacher had the wrong information about heaven with its pearly gates and streets of gold. Could it be that this was really heaven, and he just didn't recognize it for what it was?

We kids had to be roused from our prone positions on the pew and made to stand for the altar call at the end of the sermon, and upon opening our eyes, we felt isolated from the rest of the world by the blackness of the night surrounding our arbor. Relaxed as we were with Miss Ella playing a sweet, slow hymn on the traveling piano, the whole scene still remains steeped in peace and misty coated with love when I play it over in my mind.

Nightly a few worshipers would walk the dirt aisle to the awaiting preacher and others in the congregation would shed tears of thanksgiving for the joy of seeing old Tom, the town drunk, or Sister Johnson (who once left her children and her husband for three days), admit their sins and accept Jesus Christ as their Savior. Sometimes a person, whose sins were not known to the community, would make his way to the front altar and be blessed by the preacher and be therefore assured his or her name would not only be recorded in the "good book" at Heaven's gates, but would also be quietly discussed tomorrow morning over many a plate of fried eggs and buttermilk biscuits.

The amens that had punctuated the important parts of the sermon, always easily induced by the increased volume of the preacher's voice, were replaced with shouts of Hallelujah as each new Christian was prayed over and introduced to the congregation as their new Brother or Sister in God's family. Sometimes, when I had been particularly bad that day, I would consider walking that dirt path to the preacher and request him to ask God to forgive me for my mischief. But, as I got older and became a seasoned participant in weekly altar calls at our regular church services, I realized that if I were truly sorry for my sins, I could remain standing pressed close to Momma and she would understand from the tears that ran freely down my face that I intended to behave better tomorrow, and she would pull me closer and risk a wink in my direction.

My older brothers would tease me, when they caught me teary eyed and away from Momma's side, by saying that I must possess a seriously wicked heart to need such a strong nightly forgiveness that made me cry like a sissy baby at the end of every service, but I didn't care. As we children rounded up the songbooks and the men secured the wagon sheet around the piano, I knew that on that night, God was pleased with me and that at least Momma and I were assured of a place in heaven!

At the Sunday-morning service, marking the last day of the revival, the teenaged boys in the crowd begged to be chosen as the ones excused from the service so they could go ahead to the "dunking hole." They were supposed to stake it off so swimmers or other such water worshipers wouldn't be in the way when the congregation came down to baptize their sinners and wash their sins away. The chosen two or sometimes three lucky boys knew they could sneak a swim and be dried and dressed again before the congregation arrived, with only their wet hair attesting to their Sunday swim. Appointments as guards of the water hole was definitely the best job available at the revival, especially if you got to miss the entire Sunday-morning service and the ladies weighed you down with ample food for a picnic.

The highlight of each service was the saving of souls and the marrow of the message received was the comforting knowledge that now *all* the people in our little community would be welcomed inside heaven's gates. "Dinner on the grounds" was considered the grand finale. Though the women had gotten up way before dawn to fry the chicken or had stayed up late the night before cooking the pies when the house was a little cooler, it was well worth the extra effort to get the meringue just right! A good cook was as prized as a rancher's Hereford bull and this meal could well elevate a woman to what she considered her proper place in the community.

A woman's looks would not matter if her food won the admiration of the other women gathered at the Sunday dinner. No one would compare her to slim Verna Sue (who had birthed only one child in comparison to her four), or to fair-skinned and blue-eyed Dorothy Jean (who had only moved to the country a few years ago and had not spent her whole life hoeing in the garden or canning in the kitchen over a hot stove). Good cooks were elevated to queens at the Sunday dinner.

Each husband recognized his wife's serving bowls and platters and had been reminded (on the way to the arbor that morning) of the special dishes his wife had prepared. His instructions for the morning included insuring that the family arrived early enough to find a shady spot to park the car and he was charged with securing a shaded spot on one of the homemade tables for his wife's special dishes. The head of the family knew he had best remember that no matter how great the sample of another woman's cooking tasted, he didn't dare make much to do over it, or he might as well go ahead and sample her kisses for all the trouble he would be in when they got home from the revival! When the women removed the cloths covering the array of the best food found in the county that day, husbands politely took a little helping from the other cooks' bowls and a large helping from their own wife's food.

Bellies were filled to bursting, recipes were swapped, and someone would once more repeat the story about the time that it took a chicken's egg sent from the heavens to stop a wound-up revival preacher. He had insisted on trying to weed out the sinners who felt they had already been hoed enough during the last service. A chicken hen, proudly proclaiming herself wondrous after laying another perfect egg, started cackling from her nest in the willow branches above. The louder the preacher preached, the louder the chicken cackled. The hungry and tired congregation ignored the preacher and turned their attention toward the ceiling, trying to locate the chicken. With all gazes looking upward, no one missed the sight of the perfect white egg as it dropped through the arbor ceiling into the lap of a surprised Grandma Robison. The preacher had to give up that day on bringing forth any more sinners and closed the revival service with a prayer barely heard over the giggling of the worshipers.

As the babies were lulled to sleep by the heat of the afternoon, and the ranchers wished they could doze for just a few minutes in the comfort of their pickup seats, we children stood impatiently at the preacher's side awaiting our nickels for the week's worth of handing out songbooks. While the tables were being dismantled and the benches and piano were returned to their proper church homes, the revived worshipers loaded up their food baskets and ate an unwanted second dessert of dust stirred up by the long row of cars in the procession headed toward the baptizing hole.

The teenaged boys with their slicked-back and damp hair would have cleared away the weeds and brush from an area large enough for a group of Christians to walk down into either a mud-bottomed tank or a spring-fed pool, depending on the rain or the lack of it before the revival week. The observers standing along the bank wondered if the pint-sized preacher, faced with the task of immersing a gallon-sized person, could hold up to his job. Slick-bottomed tanks and slimy rocked creeks made it necessary that a deacon always stood nearby in case he was needed to rescue the baptized or the baptizer.

After they were baptized, the clothes of the wet men and women clung tightly to their bodies as they trudged their way back to the safety of the creek bank and a shawl or some other type of covering would be quickly placed around a woman's shoulders, as every precaution was taken to keep the ceremony modest. We children wished we were either the preacher or the newly saved sinner so we could have an excuse to submerge ourselves in what appeared to be a blessed relief from the heat. Perhaps next year, we told ourselves, we should go down front to meet the preacher and claim we were so sinful, we needed baptizing again.

If there were no service that Sunday night, people hugged each other and declared that this was the best revival they had ever attended and the families would go home. Supper that night on the farm would be a lonely affair after all the emotional and heartwarming nights shared with the other worshipers. I hated to part company with the other children as we always had a great time during a revival. I tried hard to keep from parting with my nickel and held onto it until it would burn such a hole in my pocket that I had to spend it at the store.

The leaves on the willow branches dried up and blew away in a few days after we left the arbor and it would stand patiently waiting until the community needed its shade to revive them again. I've heard it said that if you walk out underneath the patchy shade of what is left of that old brush arbor where our families rejoiced each year, and let your ears grow accustom to the country sounds of life, you can still hear faint voices singing the chorus of "Revive Us Again." I've also heard people say that if you listen really hard, you can hear a chicken hen cackling above the raised voice of a preacher begging sinners to walk the aisle toward Jesus.

As Patty Cakes, I considered that nickel my biggest reward for attending the revivals, but looking back as an adult, I knew that I came away from that old brush arbor with a lot more than a million shiny nickels could ever buy. I still think that maybe the preacher didn't recognize heaven when he saw it.

Safety in my mother's arms was still possible, as Momma, in her early eighties, sat beside me most days and edited my stories as I wrote. Her love of God and her writing skills were evident in everything I put on paper, for without her influence, direction, and corrections, I would be a lost soul searching for my voice. Each time we stole a few minutes to write, the awakening Christian voice inside me was revived by her unstoppable faith. Understanding my great passion to put pen to paper, she served as my slightly wrinkled cheerleader each time I finished a chapter.

Though, as with any mother, watching her child struggle with cancer was difficult. There were times when I would catch her staring at me when she thought I wasn't looking. "Momma," I asked one day, "what do you see when you look at me?"

Smiling, as if a beam of light illuminated her lovely old face, she answered, "I see a beautiful sight."

"How's that possible? I have no hair! I resemble a sad-faced, very red and very plump Maraschino cherry with sunken eyes!"

"Patty Cakes," she said with a hint of impatience, "I can't even make out your features. You're hidden in the shadow of God's protective hands, as he holds you tight."

Her words made me feel safe, as if I was small enough again to curl up in her arms under the old brush arbor. Later, as I searched the Bible for an ending scripture for a new chapter, I came across the one that Mother referred to:

> *In the shadow of His hands He hid me, he made me into a polished arrow and concealed me in his quiver.*
> ISAIAH 49:2

Chapter 12

Gifts of Pink

Courage is the price that life extracts for granting peace. The soul that knows it not, knows no release.
— Amelia Earhart

Michael was working long hours as a Drill Sergeant leaving Sharla to care completely for sick little Abigail. Nothing seemed to agree with her stomach and she had to sleep propped up because of reflux. All alone with her first baby, half-way across the United States from her family, Sharla did her best to care for Abby. Placing her in a carrier strapped around her body, Sharla packed Abby from room-to-room inside a small military-housing unit. They needed me, but I was getting weaker with each chemo infusion and the doctors would not allow me to fly while taking chemotherapy. I alternated between crying for what I couldn't do and typing furiously, the only thing I could do. God's patience must have been worn thin by my dramatic antics.

Thanksgiving was lonesome without Sharla and her family. Christmas drew near and thankfully I received my only wished for present: Sharla, Michael, and Abigail were coming home for the holidays! I was so excited that I couldn't concentrate on serious writing, so instead, I wrote a string of thank-you cards that were long overdue for gifts received during my illness.

Wearing a warm knitted cap while entwined in a pink matching scarf, I penned the giver a note. As I wrote, my feet were encompassed in a pair of raccoon house shoes complete with battery-operated heaters, both items sent by friends who knew I always felt cold. Family members contributed a breast-cancer fairy now suspended overhead and a pink survivor teddy bear sat within easy reaching distance. In the window beside my desk hung a replica of the breast-cancer ribbon made of stained glass. Pink was fast becoming a color of comfort.

Finishing my task, I made a list of people who needed Christmas presents. I had decided, without consulting anyone, that if I could go to church wearing a mask and be safe from germs, I could venture out into public to shop. I informed Eddie of my plans. You would have thought I wanted to fly solo across the Atlantic Ocean. Normally a man of few words, he surprised me by listing ten reasons why I shouldn't go. Assuring him I was not Amelia Earhart off on a dangerous flight, and that I would return in a few short hours, I put on my favorite leopard hat, placed a clean mask over my face, and went shopping.

How best could I explain what happened the day I ventured out to do my Christmas shopping? People were hurrying and scurrying wherever I went, trying their best to find the perfect present. But when they got near me at a crowded counter or passed by with their family in tow, something unforeseen happened. They felt pity for the woman battling cancer who apparently was determined to buy presents to place under her Christmas tree. Thinking about their healthy bodies, they would forget their tired feet, their dwindling cash, and Aunt Jane, who they hated to waste money on, and be thankful that they were not in my shoes.

At first, I felt odd and ducked my head so I couldn't see the pity in their eyes. Then I thought about how we needed to be reminded of how lucky we were when all was going right in our lives, and I started holding their gazes for a few seconds. By the end of the day, I looked them squarely in the eyes and smiled behind my mask, letting them see the pink skin where sideburns and eyebrows should have been. I watched them pull their family closer as they realized, that for the Grace of God, they could be me, while I thanked God for allowing me the strength to walk beside the other Christmas shoppers.

Standing in line at check-out counters, children often asked me, much to the humiliation of their mothers, why I wore a mask. I told them people gave me candy just like they did on Halloween and this usually satisfied their curiosity. When an adult was brave enough to ask about my condition, I made sure she understood that the only reason I was walking among them that day was due to God's Grace and the early detection of breast-cancer at my annual mammogram screening. Listening to my short narrative, two vendors at our local craft show presented me with gifts that I tried in vain to refuse. One was a twelve-inch cross, the other a tinkling silver wind chime. Not only was I enjoying being out in public, I had two extra gifts to hand out at Christmas!

The only problem I had was Eddie. In his logical way of thinking, I was being illogical by mixing with the other Christmas shoppers. Nothing I said could make him agree with me that I was keeping up my end of the bargain I made with God. Every time I left the house, his dire prediction of what virus I would catch followed me. Thankfully, none of them ever came true.

Christmas holidays came quickly. The children drove the long way back to Texas. Michael was skin-and-bones from all the time he spent in the field with his troops and his civilian clothes hung off of him. Sharla, too, was skinny. Not only had she lost the weight from pregnancy, she had also lost fifteen pounds from constantly bouncing Abby up and down in her carrier. It was hard not to cry out in anger when I realized how very much she had needed help from her mother. Damn, the breast cancer! I was sick of it running my life!

Calming myself, I lifted the blanket off of Abby in her car seat: I gasped at what I saw. The baby was huge! Only a few months old, but already crowding the sides of the carrier. I must have asked, "Where's Abby?" because Michael laughingly answered, "This baby ate her." Knowing he was joking, but still finding it hard to believe that this was really the tiny baby who left Texas, I turned to Sharla.

"Yes, Momma, that's Abby. She's happiest when she's nursing a bottle."

As if on cue, Abby opened her eyes and looked at me. Yep, she was Sharla's baby, there was no doubt about it; they shared the same color of crystal blue eyes. My pink Christmas present had arrived.

Ten days of wonderful followed. The house was full of people, presents, and good food. Abby was very much attached to her parents but let me hold her a little more each day. By the time they drove out the ranch gate to start their trip home, she and I had bonded.

The pictures taken at our Christmas celebration show big smiles on all our faces. That is, except for the one taken when I opened my last gift from the entire family; not just our children, but also my sister's and brother's family. Pulling back the white tissue inside the top of a large box, I found myself looking at pink material. It was a quilt to hang on the wall, made of fifteen pink and fifteen white blocks sewn together in a checkerboard pattern. The pink blocks were identical with a pink satin breast-cancer ribbon hand sewn on. The white blocks were all different. Each family, within our family, had decorated a block, some with their pictures, some with scriptures, but every name of every person in the family was written on these blocks.

Confused, I couldn't say anything. The only breast-cancer quilt I'd come across was one in a cancer clinic. It had dead women's names stitched on each block. Did my family know something I didn't? Had they been talking to my doctors and my demise was soon to come? The camera captured my stunned expression. Stuttering around, I finally managed a thank you and complimented the art work and the sewing.

Noting my hesitation in thanking them for the quilt, Stella came to my rescue. She said her daughter-in-law, Linda, had found the pattern for the quilt in a magazine. The entire family had been in on the designs and the mailing of the pieces to secure the finished blocks from distant relatives. Karon, our brother's wife, had lovingly sewn it together.

Not getting the expected reaction, Stella tried again. "Linda found the pattern to your survivor quilt in a magazine and bought all the material to make it."

A survivor quilt? Why didn't somebody say something sooner? What a great idea, a quilt for the living instead of the dead! The next time the camera caught the bald-headed woman in its lens, she wore a big smile. From that day forward, the quilt went everywhere I went. We even had our picture made together for the local newspaper. When I was pretty sure the entire community, plus all my doctors and nurses had seen it, I hung it on a quilt rack beside my bed.

At night when I couldn't go to sleep, I'd turn from side-to-side, seeking things on which to concentrate. On Eddie's dresser was the picture of me with my long hair the day I had it cut off. On my wall space, the pink quilt glowed in the soft glow of the night light. If I lay real still and stared at my picture, I swear, I could see her winking, as if she knew all along that I was loved by so many people in just my family that it would take fifteen quilt blocks to record all their names.

She is clothed with strength and dignity,
She can laugh at the days to come.
PROVERBS 31:25

Chapter 13

Got'cha

Remember, Ginger Rogers did everything Fred Astaire did, but she did it backwards and in high heels.
                                                    Faith Whittlesey

At a very early age, the two rascals I had for older brothers taught me to walk pigeon-toed and then, as soon as I could repeat a verse or two of a song, taught me the alphabet backward. Today, I still have a problem with one of my feet turning inward and remembering the proper alphabetical order of the letters N and M, or is it M and N? The first caused problems only if I attempted to run and the latter caused problems with my address book and filing of papers at the office. Yet, both of these I consider minor annoyances in life compared to the belief my brothers programmed into my head as soon as I understand somewhat, the difference between boys and girls.

My brothers had quietly informed me that they were both born little girls just like me, and had continued to be girls until their tenth birthday. On that important day, they were given the choice of magically changing into the fine specimen of boys they were today or remaining a stinky girl.

They said Momma used to dress them in pink frilly dresses and they too had conducted tea parties with their very own baby dolls. When I questioned them about why did they look like little boys in the family portrait that was taken way back before I was even born, their explanation made plenty of sense. When they changed from girls to boys, every picture taken of them in the past also changed.

They made it clear that the biggest decision I would ever have to make would be if I wanted to proceed in life as a girl or switch genders when offered the chance. It was a wonder I'm not as loony as a bird with all the hours I spent carrying on conversations in my head, my deep "boy" voice talking to my shrill "girl" voice as the two listed the pros and cons of being boys or girls. The early lists tallied inside my head held such items as girls got to play with dolls and boys got to play with lizards, with later lists including the fact that girls had to take more baths than boys and in general must stay cleaner. I liked lizards and hated baths so I swayed toward becoming a boy most of the time.

Each year as I got older and closer to my tenth birthday, I worried more than the previous year about making the right decision or more so, making the wrong one. It never occurred to me that my brothers might be lying as I was completely brainwashed by age three and I considered them close cousins to the wise men who found Baby Jesus without a map. I absorbed their every word and followed them around constantly; thus answering the question as to why my brothers picked on me so much of the time.

The summer before my birthday, I got a little reprieve from all the worrying as I was asked to spend the summer with Stella and brother-in-law, Bill. Along with their two small children, Debbie and Billy, we visited a dude ranch in Colorado for a couple of weeks. Once there, I forgot all about my upcoming decision as I was busy learning two very important lessons in life. One was how not to fly fish.

The first morning of fishing in the cool mountain air, at a pond situated in picturesque scenery and surrounded by my loving family, I accidentally hooked Bill in the lip with the fly! Although, he made light of it, it must have hurt him terribly because it bled a lot after Stella finally managed to get the hooks loose. From then on, the family pretty much stayed on the opposite side of the fishpond and ducked when I yelled "Got'cha" while casting.

The second lesson came about because I, of course, became bored with fishing by myself. No other kids my age resided at the ranch so I looked for the next best thing besides an animal to converse with: old people. I gravitated to old people partly because they always seemed to find something good to say about you and also because they didn't spend their time correcting your grammar or asking you to sit up straighter as my immediate family did. I found an old man, probably in his fifties, who was in charge of the maintenance of the dude ranch, and he set out to show me what I assumed every child wanted to know when they visited Colorado: how do you catch one of those little chipmunks?

Following his directions, I caught the first chipmunk in record time but the old man was right, I couldn't even pet the dang thing! He said the females bit more than the males and that I wouldn't be able to make a pet of one because even though they were little in stature, they were for the most part full-grown and set in their wild animal ways. The trapping had been easy as the chipmunk had darted under my shoebox to retrieve a peanut and I had simply pulled on the string attached to a little stick that was propping up the box on one end. Down came the box around the chipmunk and I carefully slid the long lid underneath it. I could hear the chipmunk darting around and around trying to get out of the box, but I held it tightly closed. "Got'cha!" I proudly said out loud.

The chipmunk would try its best to get out of the shoe box when I turned up a corner to peek inside and try even harder to sink its little sharp teeth in my hand if I tried to pet it. My right thumb already had a series of holes in it from what I suspected must be a female residing in my shoebox. I wanted to catch a male and see if he would be more affable but I had a dilemma. Where could I put this female while I attempted to catch another? I couldn't let her go in case she was the only one I ever caught and I was bound and determined to take at least one back to Texas. How impressed my normally unimpressionable brothers would be with my new pet!

I was used to catching lizards and horny toads and had come prepared with a couple of little match boxes in case one crossed my path, but so far the smallest thing I had seen to play with besides one porcupine was the chipmunks. I needed a big box or better yet, a wire cage. I searched all over the dude ranch unsuccessfully for any type of container before wandering into the cabin and opening what few cabinets and closets were inside. My suitcase might work but the chipmunk wouldn't get enough air.

Finally I caught sight of the old set of chest of drawers in my bedroom. The drawer with my soft socks, panties, and pajamas would do perfectly. I deposited my first chipmunk in the drawer and then two more chipmunks by the end of the day. The three had plenty of room to run around and I put a little jar of water in the drawer and fed them peanuts still in the shell so that they could have the fun of shelling their own, you know, more like really being in the wild! By the time we went back to Texas, I would surely have found something suitable to transport them in.

They seemed contented enough in the drawer and I named them Susie, Chip, and Dale, as I was pretty sure by their attitudes that two of them were boys. At least the last two seemed sweeter and if I didn't mind a few more "not so hard bites" I could pick them up for a second or two. I spent as much time as possible in my room claiming to be reading but actually trying to tame down the little critters. I didn't see any use in capturing any more if these three wouldn't become my friends.

The second day of the trio's captivity, our family went into Denver and spent the day shopping and sightseeing and I noticed that chiggers had made themselves at home around the elastic of my underwear. The third day our family spent visiting relatives who lived close by and I began to itch in places not proper for children to scratch in public. The fourth day the chipmunks resided in my underwear drawer our family hung around the ranch and fished and by noon of that day, I didn't care who saw me scratch or where! I had to have some relief and finally told my sister about my itching.

Based on what few facts my sister knew about my need to scratch, she decided I was allergic to the laundry soap and thought it was best if we washed all my clothes over again. Sending me into the bathroom to soak in the tub, she failed to ask my permission to open my dresser drawers. Now you have to understand that my sister had left home years before and did not grow up with two older brothers as I did. She failed to understand the fun of possessing live animals or creepy crawly things and she wasn't at all pleased when the three chipmunks scrambled past her and ran loose in the cabin. You could have heard her scream all the way in Texas!

Boy was I in trouble! Not only had live critters been sleeping in the same house as us humans, which was completely unacceptable, but also these live critters were apparently infested with mites or fleas or both. Luckily for me, I didn't catch whatever disease the parasites crawling on the chipmunks carried. Yet, to this day, if I start to tell my chipmunk story, I hear about how bad the bubonic plague was back then and how I nearly could have caught it and how I nearly could have died, and how many of my family members I nearly could have killed! My argument about the whole episode was since I never saw the chipmunks scratching, how could I be to blame for the infestation of my body and the cabin?

Of course, I don't need to put in writing what the second lesson was I learned that summer. Funny thing though, for about a week while still itching and as I tried to go to sleep at night, I could hear a little "chattery" voice saying, "Got'cha!"

Summer abruptly came to an end and since my tenth birthday was in October, time was running out for me to make up my mind what sex I wanted to be for the rest of my life. I couldn't sleep for worrying and it was hard to concentrate the first month of school that year. I was in turmoil all through September—boy, girl? Boy, girl? What did I want to be in life? Be like my sweet sister or like my crazy brothers? The latter had a lot more fun.

October finally came and so did my answer. An early birthday present arrived in the form of a book, Harper Lee's *To Kill a Mockingbird*, and I knew when I finished reading it what I wanted to do in life. I wanted to be an author just like Harper Lee and write a novel so full of motion and emotion that nobody would want to put down the book. Not realizing Harper Lee was of the female gender, I would ask to be magically transformed into a boy. (Everyone knew girls didn't have a chance of succeeding in the literary field.)

Frightened of my decision, I lay in bed at night trying to remember boy things, like how to tie a lure on a fishing line or how to spit far enough to make it over the porch railing. Football and baseball knowledge surely came along with the change, but I couldn't really be sure so I needed to ask my brothers for more details about my upcoming transformation.

Of course, when I asked for more information just two days before my tenth birthday, my now teenage brothers had long ago forgotten they had even told me such a tale! You should have heard them hoop and holler when I asked about the knowledge of sports appearing at the same time the switch occurred! My face was still red on my birthday and continued to flush with heat for a long time if one of them walked up behind me and whispered, "Got'cha!"

As it turned out, I would have made the wrong decision for the wrong reason anyway as Harper Lee's novel won a Pulitzer Prize and became an Academy Award winning film. That was when I discovered Harper Lee was a girl!

I wouldn't be stretching the truth by saying the stinkers I had for brothers offered me countless opportunities to overcome obstacles. At least my childhood experiences gave me plenty to write about besides cancer. Maybe my next undertaking will be purely fictional, centered on my life after I changed into a boy. *I'll have plenty of time won't I, Lord, after I say "Got'cha" to the breast cancer?*

> *For if the willingness is there, the gift is acceptable according to what one has, not according to what he does not have.*
> 2 CORINTHIANS 8:12

Chapter 14

One-Woman Parade

> *Guided by my heritage of a love of beauty and respect for strength—in search of my mother's garden, I found my own.*
>
> — Alice Walker

In the 1950s, my daddy ran off with a woman named Dimples, taking my two brothers with him. Mother couldn't stand to be separated from her sons, so she borrowed enough money for the move, packed up her two girls, and left Texas following the males of our family to the small sand-coated town of Carlsbad, New Mexico. Mother's courage and strength to follow her heart eventually succeeded in the reuniting of our family, but those few years were the roughest that our family had to endure.

In a town where all the surroundings were the color of sand, Momma found us a place to live. We moved into a house so tiny that the double bed all of us shared had to be folded up inside a closet during the day to allow room for us to move around. I was always fascinated by the impressive two-story house facing the main street that was directly in front of our little home—which was originally servant's quarters.

In lieu of paying rent, my teenage sister was expected to clean the owner's big house on the weekends while our mother struggled to provide money for our other necessities. After the first couple of Saturdays, I refused to go along to help Stella even though the big house had the first television set that I had ever seen. But, the television set did little to tame my nerves since I was terrified of the old man with a hunched back who resided in one of the upstairs bedrooms. He would inch down the stairs with his body bent over as if he needed to see his belly button in order to walk.

In making sure no harm befell me, my mother arranged for my brothers to come watch me while Mother and Sister worked. My brothers reasoned that in order to keep me really safe from harm, they should capture me at least once a day, place me on the bed, fold me up into the wall, and shut the closet doors. I would, of course, end up sliding down between the wooden back wall and the mattress. After a couple of these "safety drills," I soon learned which way to turn when they threw me up on the bed. Otherwise, I would be standing on my head when the bed settled itself against the back wall.

Locked inside the closet, deep within the wall of the house, I learned patience. I stood quietly in the dark listening to their laughter and their jokes about flat-faced girls who couldn't wear glasses and flat-chested girls who couldn't wear sweaters. Those two boys were positively sure that I had no room between the wall and the mattress. Little did they know!

Later, my brothers would become *greatly* concerned about me and beat on the closet doors while yelling my name. I would stand silently and wait them out. By keeping perfectly quiet, I would speed up their curiosity and they would check on me sooner, which meant escape! I did not dare get sleepy during my confinement because when the bed started to unfold, I would have to climb back up on it by holding onto the covers, or the bottom half of me would really get flattened between the wall and the metal headboard when the bed came to rest again on the floor. Patiently, I waited until their guilt overcame them and I could hear them agreeing to let me out. Thank God we didn't have a television set like the owners of the big house or I would have been forgotten for hours. I must admit the ride up and down while grasping the bed covers was really quite fun—although the imprisonment was quite scary.

My two big brothers had me convinced that if I told anybody about being shut up in the bed closet, the bottoms of my feet would turn black and for the rest of my life anyone who saw my bare feet would know I was just a plain old "scaredy cat!" I kept my mouth shut. Besides, Mother's nerves were already at the breaking point and we had learned to settle our problems between ourselves.

I was now thankful for the time alone in the bed closet, since the saying goes that all lessons learned in our early years are lessons that stay with us for life. This early childhood lesson enabled me to exhibit a tremendous amount of patience since the incident paralleled my *cancer* closet; all alone with my fears of what tomorrow might bring. I could sit for hours in a waiting room hidden behind a mask worn to ward off other people's germs, wearing a hat to cover my bald head, and work a crossword puzzle until the cows came home (or when the nurse finally called my name). These brotherly love episodes let me patiently wait for slumber while I lay in my bed at night and listened to my husband sleep peacefully. In fact, I had to have more patience waiting for my hair to sprout new growth than I ever did while in that dark closet waiting for my brothers to release me.

Finally, my hair was coming back in! The second series of chemo was not as intense as the first and my bald-time was cut in half: four months of wearing a wig instead of eight. I could run a comb flat against my head and my hair was long enough to show itself on the topside of the comb. I caught myself in front of the mirror several times a day just looking at my emerging hair; touching it. I sometimes pretended that I could see it growing. Would my hair be mostly gray or mostly brown, curly instead of straight again? I'd take hair anyway it grew! Patience paid off.

I seemed to need to show my fuzzy head to everyone I met and lifted my hat and flashed my proud grin, and said, "Look, it's coming back in!" I scared at least two or three people by my sudden outbursts and the baring of my head. I probably really did confuse, or amuse, a few people on Valentine's Day when I went hatless and proudly displayed a heart on the entire backside of my fuzzy head, outlined with brown eyeliner and colored in with pink lipstick. For once, I didn't mind if the locals talked about my one-woman parade around town, as I had to share this rebirth of my hair. If I didn't give it a proper welcoming, it would either fall out again or withdraw into my scalp and I would awaken and be bald again. My patience would not make it waiting for hair to grow the second time!

Mother, unlike me, had no brothers or sisters and she never had patience deep-seated in her soul at an early age. I was glad she became restless while waiting for daddy to grow tired of Dimples (the love affair dragged on for years). My mother's one-woman parade gave me the strength to walk mine. On one very stressful day, Mother lost what little patience she possessed, along with her temper, and finally set things right.

Daddy was the jealous one of my two parents. When a male acquaintance of Mother's began to pay her some attention, "saintly" Daddy stupidly confronted her about it. My parents' encounter was at the hospital where my oldest brother was engaged in another life-threatening battle from complications of his hemophilia. Emotions were at a peak. Momma already had enough to worry about when Daddy had the gall to voice his accusations of Momma caring for this particular man. After all, Daddy was married to Dimples!

Sweet Momma forgot her ladylike upbringing and surprised the people gathered in the hall around my brother's hospital room. She took off one of her red pointed high heels, held it firmly in her right hand, and clobbered my daddy in the head, causing a fair-sized hole to appear in his skull. Daddy was admitted to the hospital for observation.

No one blamed Momma for the damage she caused to Daddy's head. As it turned out, Momma ended up taking both her men home to her house after they had recovered. She won the battle that had been raging between lust and family love. Because of her, our little family of six was reunited. My parents lived nearly sixty years together before my daddy passed away.

No wonder I've always talked to the Lord as if he and I were friends because I was raised by a mother who believed true faith in the Lord would bring its own rewards. I watched her work her way through many trials and tribulations in her lifetime and her faith still preceded her every step. I also knew that battles worth winning were not won overnight. Hair did not grow back while you watched for it in the mirror. The bottoms of your feet didn't turn black when you admitted to being a scaredy cat.

> *I can do everything through him who gives me strength.*
> PHILIPPIANS 4:23

Chapter 15

Lost on a Clear, Bright, Sunshiny Day

Courage is not the towering oak that sees storms come and go; it is the fragile blossom that opens in the snow.
—Alice M. Swaim

When my brother Doug was twelve, I was six. No matter how much I grew in any given year, he was always bigger and smarter than I was and he took advantage of this, as all children with younger siblings will do. He used to take me out in the pasture at Grandma Flossie's farm and make me close my eyes while he turned me 'round and 'round until I was practically falling down with dizziness. Then he would point and tell me the way back to the house was yonder and insist I go on home so he could go off hunting by himself as supposedly a tag-a-long little sister made too much noise, and I would sulk off and let him be.

Eventually after I had walked the full length of the one hundred acre farm and found only the back perimeter fence instead of Grandma's house, I would realize he had confused my sense of direction by first turning me in circles and then telling me north was south.

Finding my way back would take longer if the day was cloudy, as I needed to navigate my safe return to the farmhouse by using the location of the sun. I learned early on that it was easier to plot your return back to a familiar path if you got lost on a clear, bright, sunshiny day.

Sometimes he'd make me steal five or six long matches from the tin box Grandma Flossie had hanging on the kitchen wall. We would go a long piece from the house where my grandparents couldn't smell the smoke and he would build a little fire and proceed to kill a bird with whatever gun or slingshot he had on him at the time. Bird dead, he'd pull out its feathers and tell me to hold the bloody thing until he could find just the right sticks to build a primitive roasting spit. It required two strong sticks with forked ends and one straight stick, whittled to a point that was sharp enough on one end to ram through the poor little dead bird.

Now this ramming stick wasn't just any stick you picked up off the ground and set to whittling on. No, it had to be a green stick; a growing limb severed only minutes before it pierced the bird's entrails. Oh, and the entrails? Well, he never really gutted the bird and the organs, and whatever else gunk was inside the bird, stayed in the bird. That is, all but what got poked out when he pushed the stick through. It was a pretty gory way to cook, but that wasn't the bad part.

The bad part was I always "got" to sample the meat when Doug decided it was done. Sometimes the bird cooked for only a few short minutes because Grandpa Bob's big bull was headed in our direction or maybe the bird endured ten or fifteen minutes of roasting until it turned good and black. No matter the long or short of the cooking, I was always the guinea pig and let me tell y'all, if you've never tasted a bird roasted on a green stick, it's pretty bad stuff. It's a flavor you never forget! I could possibly have refused but Doug's insistent, "Eat it, Patty Cakes, or I'll tell Grandma Flossie you stole the kitchen matches," was usually reason enough for me to sample the roasted bird.

Surviving my younger years made me strong. Probably stronger than most little girls who wore dresses even in the summer and went to ballet practice or swimming parties instead of staying at their grandparents' in the country and carrying out daily chores such as gathering the chicken eggs. Chinning yourself up to look in a hen's wooden laying box mounted on the wall of a smelly and shadowy chicken house was tough stuff because you never knew what you were going to come eye-to-eye with, but you were darn sure something dangerous was waiting in that box. We always had to watch for snakes!

Hens about to be robbed of their eggs were always on the defensive and sliding your hand under the hen while her little beady eyes stared you down and her sharp pointed beak sat poised and ready to strike were horrors enough. But if you were so unlucky to attempt your egg thievery at the same time a big chicken snake became hungry for eggs, protective hens were the least of your worries. What always got me hurt was running in circles inside the chicken house, trying to remember where the gap was in the chicken wire that served as the door, so I could get the heck away from that snake! I would return to the house eggless and scratched in a zillion places from attempting to make a new hole for a faster exit from the chicken house. I hated to gather eggs!

For most of this past year while I had been fighting my battle with cancer and because of one of the bosses who used intimidation to rule, my workplace environment had been a cross between the unforgettable "gaggable" taste of a dead bird roasted on a green stick and chinning yourself up every day to see what new horrors were nesting in the wooden box on a chicken-coop wall. Plus, with the endless mounds of graphs and charts that he manipulated to show how far the business was in jeopardy of failing unless he was allowed to take over the reins and save it, he made a brilliant attempt to confuse me and the other people in charge, and send us down the wrong road. I had no idea how the rest of the staff coped with his constant attempt to reorganize the entire company to suit himself.

I had been fighting two battles instead of just one, as it became more and more apparent that he was building a case against me. I told myself that nothing he could dole out could be as frightening as some of the places I had found myself in, but could not convince myself that I would end up both cancer free and still be employed. I was ashamed that my faith was greatly shaken and admit that I spent equal time thanking God for my job and then turning right around and worrying that my job would be taken away.

I could only hope that when the snake finally showed his head and I was left to find my way back from the spot of what he considers a place of no return, that it occurred on a clear, bright, sunshiny day. With God's radiant light to guide me, I'd find a way to return to where I belonged.

> *The Lord is my light and my salvation—whom shall I fear? The Lord is the stronghold of my life—of whom shall I be afraid.*
>
> PSALM 27:1

Chapter 16

Devil at My Door

You gain strength, courage and confidence by every experience in which you really stop to look fear in the face. You are able to say to yourself, "I lived through this horror. I can take the next thing that comes along." ... You must do the thing you think you cannot do.
ELEANOR ROOSEVELT 1884 – 1962

On a crisp, cool April day, my world turned into a state of pure panic. Okay, so I had seen warning flags of impending danger, but had been simply too tired to do much about heading off the storm. That day, like so many before, I wore a black straw hat that framed my round flushed face like a dark shadow surrounding a plump red tomato, a face red and swollen from the many doses of steroids that I had taken along with my eight infusions of chemotherapy. I was physically weak from my battle to insure that the cancer cells were not roaming freely through my body or hosting a silent picnic with my organs.

Finally, I had finished my last dose of chemo and was expecting to get my strength back anytime now. What would it feel like to have normal energy again? Could I even remember?

Although I had missed only a couple of days of work with each chemo infusion, the total of all the days I had been out with surgeries, doctors' appointments, blood work, etc., had been numerous and my sick-leave days had dwindled to barely enough left to schedule my reconstruction surgery. I was at work that day only because I sternly chastised myself that morning until I sluggishly arose from my soft bed, my sanctuary; the only place where I didn't have to act brave and confident, determined and strong.

Today I was tired, but considered this merely an inconvenience in my winning battle over the treacherous cancer cells. As on so many times before, I sat at my desk working on the end-of-the-month reports when I heard the meeting breaking up in the boardroom. I looked up and saw Daemon, the board member I feared the most, and the company lawyer standing just outside my office door, deep in conversation. They entered silently and shut the door behind them. Fear dripped over me like slow pouring molasses. I knew what was about to happen but as they sat across from me, I prayed fervently that I was mistaken.

These two men were probably uncomfortable at the sight of me without eyebrows or eyelashes, or any sideburns to peep out from underneath my hat as chemotherapy works by killing all the fast-growing cells in your body, which includes of course, every hair you possess. Looking like one of those hairless show cats that win all the awards, even I would glance at myself in the mirror and ask, *"Who is this person staring back at me?"*

With only fuzzy snatches of hair that resembled goose-down dotting the top of my hat-covered head, I felt as vulnerable and sacrificial as a plucked chicken waiting for the boiling pot. There was no place for me to run, no back door in my office that would allow me to escape, no wooden tunnel door with Jesus waiting with outstretched hands for my knock. I was alone with the man I feared the most...and a lawyer. *May God be with me.*

In the years I had worked for this company, I had many bosses, seven at a time, and they had been varied in personalities and business backgrounds. The majority of them believed that if nothing was broken, they should leave things alone. This meant I was able to perform my job as general manager and progress with the company through the years. With the director's guidance, our staff had managed to keep the revenue up, the expenses down, and added 3,000 customers in the last eleven years. I had always felt a strong sense of pride and accomplishment in my work and knew that I had contributed greatly along with the rest of the staff to the security of the business.

As with many people, I had gained a sense of identity through my career. I had allowed it to define who I was, and was proud of my position. I had worked years at that job, spending too much time at the office before I became ill, using that business to fill my empty nest as the last child left for college.

The thirteen employees who worked with me were handpicked and added one at a time as the company grew. Before the chemo zapped my energy, I would come to their defense in a minute if need be. I stood up for my team and knew they would do the same for me.

That day, however, my defenses and my dignity were so low they would not register on any scale. I felt suspended like a hot-air balloon waiting for the point of a sharp needle to make its jab. What was I going to do for a job when they got through with me this morning?

Our small town knew all about my cancer and I wouldn't be able to get another job in the community. No other business would want to add my health problems to their already elevated insurance rates and I couldn't blame them. And, leaving town to hunt for a job would be fruitless for several more months, as anyone with the blessing of sight would know I was battling cancer just by looking at me. *What was I going to do?*

This was so unfair! I would have stayed in bed that day if this job had not called my name at a very early hour. What would my reason be tomorrow to crawl out of bed? *I beg of you, Lord, don't let them fire me.* Where would I go? How would I manage paying for my health insurance and my reconstruction surgery?

With some preamble of his credentials to bring me such a document, Daemon handed me a page of text that pointed out my lack of managerial skills. "You have not been able to produce what was expected of you," he said, looking me straight in the eye, "and I have to tell you, Patty, there is a serious flaw in your job production. Your job performance is not acceptable to the company."

Daemon cleared his throat and continued, "As you see, the paper states that you have thirty days from the date of this letter to produce a project for the board's review and to respond to two other allegations brought forward in the document." He continued to tell me that at that meeting, one short month away, a decision would be made as to my value to the company.

My value? Did eleven years of service mean nothing? Was there no loyalty anymore in the workplace? I was screaming inside.

I was offered no hope that I would be able to retain my job. But at least I had paid health insurance for another thirty days! My mind kept repeating you don't have to go home today; you don't have to go home today!

I listened to his recital without breaking down and kept my arms crossed below what used to be two healthy breasts and sat up straight in my chair. If he looked close enough though, he would realize I was scared to death. "Daemon," I asked, "are you representing the entire seven board members?"

"Yes," he said.

"Well," I said as calmly as I could, "I just finished my last dose of chemotherapy two weeks before and would you please ask the board to take this under consideration—I have been fighting a battle with cancer for the last nine months."

He responded, "The board knows this, but you are still lacking in the areas we've listed on the page and we're giving you thirty days to produce the project, plus respond to the other problems we've outlined for you. We're being more than fair and sympathetic to your circumstances, Patty."

Fair and sympathetic? I wanted to scream and kick him. I wanted to say, *why don't you change places with me for a while and see how you feel!*

They rose and left my office while I fought to contain my anger.

I got up and closed the door and watched through the blinds until they got into their respective cars and drove away. Then, I howled at the impossibility of the task before me. I had neither the strength nor the determination to carry out his demand for a finished project. I was a goner in thirty days. At my desk I cried like the blubbering fool he had just pointed out that I was. Through my tears, I finished the work on top of my desk and tried to contain myself enough to inform the rest of the staff of the board's letter.

The other employees rallied to my defense and offered to help complete the project or better yet, help craft a defense on my behalf to the board. I hated to admit it, but told them I was too tired to fight another battle. Weary and dejected, I drove home and crawled into bed where I stayed for several days, using up a few more of my precious sick-leave days. While curled up in a fetal position with the sheet pulled over my silly-looking hair, I did a lot of thinking, and did a lot of praying. God was listening as He always is.

In those few days I got some much-needed rest. How much clearer I could think when I allowed my body and mind some down time to overcome the last chemo treatment! As soon as I could go a full day without crying, I went back to work with only twenty-five days left to meet the boss's demands.

The office engineer tried to help, but I truly believed that no matter if I did or didn't present the project in thirty days, the board would only find fault with it and all our efforts would be wasted. But the engineer would not hear of my giving in and although it went completely against my nature to allow someone else to do my job for me, he practically took over that project. The rest of the employees spent their time encouraging me and instead of standing behind me, they did more. They held me up and together we worked on the best way to respond to the other two allegations. Even the company lawyer gave me pointers on how to best prepare my response.

First, I had to face the facts concerning the allegations. I was not as "worldly wise" as my boss. I had no university or college degree to prove my value and had no experience in the "real" corporate business world of "dog eat dog." He, on the other hand, had both, and he had spent considerable time putting together a file to prove to the other six directors that funds were missing from our company.

He knew in my weakened condition I was completely at his mercy and surely thought he had me whipped. He believed that I would cower down and crawl home to the safety of my bedcovers, and that

I would not get my strength back in time to complete this project and confront the other allegations. He believed his crafty writing and accusations would win and that I was going to leave this office unemployed at the next board meeting.

Was he going to win? He had the upper hand and I was tired of all the fights during the last months. But, I was also worried that several of the other employees would be relieved of their duties if they helped me, and we all needed our incomes. I had to do something to make myself toughen up besides praying constantly so I took a piece of paper and wrote the words, *"Devil, get away from my door!"* and taped it to the back of my office door. The next weeks, whenever I lost my self-confidence, I shut the door, stared at that sign, and repeated the phrase out loud until the fear of failure left me alone.

My need to retain my health insurance and my income, plus my protective attitude toward the other employees, kept me from resigning my position. I would stay and make him be the one to terminate my employment.

The days counted down until the board meeting and I was terrified. If the ladies in the office, Danita, Petrea, and Billie Jean, had not listened to my wailing and wiped my tears away during that thirty-day time frame, I probably would have turned and fled. But real friends don't desert a sinking ship.

An agenda had to be posted for each meeting that stated what would be discussed at the public meeting. The "General Manager's Performance Review" was one of the items listed for the next meeting. The company lawyer, the board president, the administrative assistant, and I all reviewed the agenda individually before it was finalized. The words "General Manager's Performance Review" seemed to stand out from the other items. The agendas were posted at three courthouses in the counties our company serviced and man, the humiliation I felt upon realizing that I had at one time or another lived in all three of these counties. My review would not go unnoticed. When they were posted seventy-two hours in advance of the meeting, the countdown for the showdown began.

By then, I had lost my ruddy complexion and my body was not as swollen as it had been. With no more chemo in my future, I was thirty days closer to regaining my strength, but would my strength allow me to sit through a night meeting that could possibly last for hours?

Then the most amazing thing happened and if you believe in God and His miracles, you know that you may not have the answer as to how it happens. You just believe. That's why it's called a miracle.

The line item of "General Manager's Performance Review" was missing off all the agendas posted for the meeting! By law, no discussion concerning the general manager could be held at this meeting. I had miraculously been given another thirty day's reprieve! I jumped for joy! Thank you, God! Thank you!

Good things happened during the next thirty days as it was election time. Two new board members replaced two old board members, the president's seat changed into a Christian's hands and by word of mouth, news got out that I was going to be fired while trying to recover from breast cancer and its subsequent treatments. People who had never met me joined those who had and the meeting room was packed to standing room only. When time came for my review, I asked that it be made public and not held behind closed doors, which was the normal procedure. When I took the podium and read a portion of the paper I had prepared in my defense, the outcry from the public disrupted the room. I never finished reading all that I had prepared. Instead, I was allowed to sit down and rest throughout the rest of the meeting.

A bad financial decision made by a portion of the seated board that had eventually cost our business thousands of dollars became public knowledge that night—along with the discussion of a change in policy that was costly to our customers. With all the commotion in the boardroom, no decision on my review was made. I was able to have my scheduled reconstruction surgery while still employed by the company! Another miracle!

I was struggling with more than just the loss of my job. I was trying to make a decision whether or not to have my left breast removed at the same time I had reconstruction surgery. If Daemon had not been hovering over me with his allegations of mismanagement and insisting that my job performance was not acceptable, I might have kept my left breast. But, I couldn't see going through all of this again if the cancer reappeared. Eddie and I could never afford the cancer treatments without health insurance to cover the expenses. I thought it best to get it over with and go on with the rest of my life, breastless.

I did not talk to anyone about my decision and only informed the plastic surgeon the day before I was scheduled to have reconstruction surgery on my right breast. He took a good look at my determined face and tore in half the pre-operation forms that his office had prepared for my signature. When I got home that night from my doctor's visit and what few hours I had managed to work at the office, I told Eddie what I intended to do. We held each other and I cried. I felt that I had no other choice since my future at the office was not secure. Right or wrong, good decision or bad, I would always consider Daemon responsible for the loss of my other breast.

Surgery was a blur: a mastectomy, two implants placed behind my chest muscles and liposuction under both arms, all completed in less than four hours. I was home before 4:00 p.m. that same day. My family and I were greatly upset that my insurance did not allow me to spend a night in the hospital. The trauma alone of losing a breast warranted at least one night's observation by trained nurses.

I was at home recovering when the board meeting occurred the next month. They told me that the public, along with several of the board members, turned again on Daemon and voiced their displeasure with the man for various reasons. The next day, he resigned! *Thank you, God!*

Needless to say, a party ensued at my house that night as we celebrated another miracle! I waited until the guests had all gone home and Eddie was fast asleep before seeking the darkest spot in the house and praying what I hoped was a sufficient thank you to our Lord. Although it was hard for me to get down on my knees and back up again just two days after the surgery to remove my left breast and install my implants, I didn't mind the pain.

Concentrating on being thankful instead of bitter over the loss of another major part of my femininity, the next day I started on a list of thank you cards to the crowd of people who had played a role in saving my job. A huge burden had been lifted off my shoulders. I was still employed. I still had my health insurance, plus, I could quit worrying about the security I was seeking for the other employees. God had taken care of us all.

The one who recently resigned had not thought that possibly God had placed me in the position I held with the company. There was no way for that board member to know that at one time in my life, I had been close enough to smell Jesus' sweet breath. Again, I felt His arms wrapped tightly around me.

The day after Daemon's resignation, I went out on the porch of the house and took a broom handle and finished knocking down a mud swallow's nest that had been hanging by one corner for several days. I picked it up off of the concrete and noticed shiny threads of dark red entwined in the soft part of the nest. Upon examination, I discovered the dark red threads were really strands of my recently lost, long auburn hair! My habit of going out on the porch after I washed my hair and combing it and letting it blow-dry in the wind had given the birds this soft nesting material. The strands were still strong and shiny and I knew God had given me this visible sign that in the not-too-distant future, He would reinstate my physical strength and my healthy hair as easily as He had controlled my destiny at work.

Carefully, I placed the swallow's nest in the garden shed and went back into the house and looked up the verse Luke 12:24: *"Consider the ravens: They do not sow or reap, they have no storeroom or barn; yet God feeds them. And how much more valuable you are than birds!"*

I knew I'd soon retrieve the bird's nest from the garden shed to show my grandchildren the strands of my hair so lovingly and carefully preserved by one of God's little creatures. At that time in my cancer walk I might have resembled a plucked hen to those who didn't know my true heart, but in God's loving eyes, I would always be a graceful swan swimming on a clear pool of blue water. And with His love, I would be able to keep the Devil away from my door.

> *We fight with weapons that are different from those the world uses. Our weapons have power from God that can destroy the enemy's strong places.*
>
> 2 CORINTHIANS 10:4

Chapter 17

Hopscotch & Dominoes

"Let your life lightly dance on the edges of time like dew on the tip of a leaf."

RABINDRANATH TAGORE

My husband and I went to bed last night with the silence of the still and sticky stagnant air heavy around us, and awoke to the comforting sound of raindrops on the metal roof. I arose before dawn, praising the Lord for my renewed strength and the continued healing of my new chest, and listened to the sounds of the hard rain as it cascaded down our roof and tapped fervently on the windowpanes. With buttered toast in hand, I turned off the kitchen light and sat in total darkness and ate my breakfast while watching the display of lightning as it pranced across the northern horizon.

Soon, my husband would return home from his 5:00 a.m. coffee-shop detail in town, where this morning instead of fighting foreign wars while eating bakery items, they would talk of storms much worse than this that occurred way back when. Funny, this downpour of much needed rain would ruin the city folks' weekend plans while at the same time, would create a well-deserved holiday for the Texas ranchers in our area. Maybe today, he would be able to rest his always tired body, the way I had been resting mine, until the rain soaked into the parched ground and ranch duties began again, probably as early as this afternoon. So much had happened lately that I was glad to have some quiet time to sit and reminisce over other rainy days.

My grandparents' old farmhouse had a tin roof on the screened-in porch, but when rain fell the sound was deafening because there was no insulation between the tin and the ceiling. Covering our ears with our hands, we would stand just inside the safety of the kitchen door, where if lightning struck the tin porch, we would not be zapped to heaven before our time. As a young child, I leaned up against the warm and comfortable body of Grandma Flossie while the cooling rain ran like little creeks off the roof onto the sandy ground.

Sometimes if it was a slow rain and no thunder rumbled in the distance, Grandma would let us escape and we would run like wild Indians around the little farmhouse until we were soaked through and through and towels and dry clothes were in order. Making circles around that house while whooping like warriors as they chased cowboys was purely imaginative fun.

Rainy days were usually followed by a trade day with the town's local merchants as no productive farm work could be done until the ground dried out. My grandparents would load us kids and a wooden crate of chicken eggs in Grandma's little red Valiant, a car with push buttons mounted on the dash that changed the transmission gears. Why she ever chose red for her car color, I don't know, but it sure gave the bull something to chase when we took off on an adventure into town to sell the eggs. Slipping and sliding in the red sand after a downpour, with a big black bull trying to head you off before you reached the safety of the cattle guard that separated the farm road from the public dirt road, was pretty hard on a crate full of fragile chicken eggs. But it was lots of fun for us children in the back seat since in those days, we didn't have to be buckled in for our own safety. We would collide in mid air and bounce all around, giggling the whole time.

Grandma Flossie always did the driving and before the trip commenced, always took out a pair of gloves from the "glove box" and slipped them on over her work-worn hands. On the hot Texas summer days, her fast driving made you think of a red whirlwind going down a dusty road.

Once we got the eggs traded for whatever groceries she needed for the week, she took us to the nickel and dime store. On each trip she would buy us a fresh batch of plastic cowboys and Indians as we were forever burying ours in holes we dug in the sandy yard with the help of some big cast-off serving spoons. No telling how many tribes of Indians and their rival cowboys were buried in that old front yard.

After I was older and my grandparents had passed away, in winters our family had to go back there at least twice a week and take care of the cattle. Upon arrival at the cold and lifeless farmhouse, we were forced to participate in a ritual that still made me cringe today. Before the heat cast off by the one propane stove located in the living room could penetrate to the bedrooms, you had to remove the lizards and anything else alive and hibernating between the box springs and the mattresses. Momma would hold up the mattress and covers and we were instructed to grab whatever ran in our direction. Mice, lizards, snakes, spiders, and stinging scorpions cohabited if it was a dark enough area and especially in the warmest places in the house. I would often nearly faint at the sight of so many of my worst fears roosting together in the bed. I was usually delegated as the lizard catcher as I would scream less when they ran toward me.

Now, I thought little lizards were cute and I was known on occasion to save a tiny one in a little matchbox where he could keep company with a little horned toad I had captured earlier in the peanut field. But this grabbing and catching hold of frightened and cold-skinned lizards would always cause their tails to depart from their bodies and a writhing, flopping tail would be left in the palm of my hand. Nothing besides a mouse running full blast in my direction would make me shudder more than holding this piece of lizard flesh while it spent its last energy. Lord, I hated gathering lizards, but the alternative was I'd wake up in the middle of the night in my warm bed and realize I was accompanied by a cold-blooded reptile seeking my body heat.

We also had to search other areas for unwanted visitors and remove them from inside the farmhouse. Sometimes on our searches we would miss a well-hidden cold-blooded reptile and find him or her after the house warmed up. One very cold morning, Momma got up and plugged in the electric percolator and went back to bed to stay warm until it did its chore. When she got up again to pour Daddy's coffee, which she always served him in bed, she was greatly surprised by a snake that had wrapped himself around the sugar bowl, just beside the warm coffeepot. The snake, quite content with his perch, was lazily absorbing the heat. Momma, never afraid of snakes as long as she could see they were not poisonous, captured him close to his head, allowed him to wrap around her wrist and forearm, and took him outside and released him. I of course spent the next night wondering whose bed he was going to turn up in as I was quite sure he went straight back through his entrance into Grandma's house and was waiting patiently for the lights to go out again. Needless to say, I *always* tried to spend the night with someone back in town to avoid these necessary but totally scary adventures.

No television was ever brought into this farmhouse and playing with a deck of cards was considered a sin, so dominoes were our main source of entertainment. After supper and after my grandparents had read and argued their Bible study verses for that night (Grandpa was a Methodist and Grandma was a Baptist), it was time to play. You not only had to be able to correctly add spots on the dominoes, you also had to be stout enough to hold your feet suspended off the floor for the entire time you were playing. If you didn't, a scorpion would prance his way up your leg and light up your body with the poison he carried ready for battle in his curled up tail. Scorpions, being nocturnal, ruled the rooms at night and you hardly ever got up to visit the bathroom after dark unless it was a great emergency. Then, you better take as few steps as possible and look before you sat!

Patty Cakes loved to play dominoes back then and would beg to play just one more game every night before they shut off the lights. Begging partly to play for the sake of possibly winning one more hand, but mostly begging because she was afraid to go to bed where slithering things might share her pillow!

Her adult counterpart spent nearly a year putting off going to bed because of what tomorrow would bring. But I learned from my long ago childhood experiences in Grandma Flossie's house that when it was time for the lights to be doused, you were safer tucked in your bed underneath the covers. Beside my sweet husband, and under the watchful eyes of God, I found a haven from all things scary.

If sleep evaded me, I spent time in prayer and then replayed scenes of yesteryears, or possibly yesterday, a rainy day, when the grandchildren had helped me explore the ranch, two kids snapped into one adult raincoat. I hated that no lizards or horned toads were left on this place for them to chase and capture. Ah, the fun of possessing live critters so tiny that you could keep them in a small sliding match box that fit perfectly inside your blue jean pocket!

My grandchildren seem satisfied, though, with the outdoor adventures we had discovering a couple of snakes on our rounds near the stock tanks, concocting stories surrounding the various animal tracks/artifacts we located throughout the pasture, going armadillo hunting at night, and building tree houses. The grandchildren did not seem to miss at all the thrill I described to them of hop-scotching around scorpions on the trip to the bathroom while playing dominoes at night.

I expected, however, that they would laughingly tell of the day they were playing dominoes at the picnic table with their bald-headed grandmother when a repairman came down the road to the ranch house. Although he was polite enough not to stare too long, my grandchildren thought it was funny that I had forgotten I didn't have on a wig or my hat, my new hair growth barely peeping through my pink scalp. For weeks afterward, the grandchildren would ask me, "I wonder how many baldheaded grandmothers the washer repairman saw playing dominoes this week?"

Thank you, Lord, for grandchildren.

> "God has brought me laughter."
> GENESIS 21:6

Chapter 18

Sunday's Hands

The most visible joy can only reveal itself to us when we've transformed it, within.
                    RAINER MARIA RILKE

A church family became very important to us as I worked my way through the chemo treatments and we searched for a church more in tune with the "old-time religion" that Eddie and I grew up with. The search ended when we stopped and thought about which pastor was already taking care of us even though we had never indicated our need for his prayers.

After my first surgery, I had looked up from my drug induced state and found Brother Roy Smith standing at my bedside praying for my speedy recovery and possibly my soul. Eddie was busily tapping me on the shoulder, trying to warn me to open my eyes before I opened my mouth. Brother Roy became a welcomed companion for Eddie during my hospital visits.

It was wonderful to walk the aisle of Lawler Baptist Church holding hands with mother on one side and Eddie on the other. The congregation that shook our hands at the back door after the service included Martha Georg and her sisters, the Guthrie girls, who had asked us for years to join them at Lawler. We felt right at home.

Shortly after joining, I undertook a major attitude adjustment after having asked Brother Roy for counseling with the jealous streak that kept my eyes glowing green in certain circumstances. Telling our new pastor, expecting him to offer me some hints to ease my pain, I was quite taken back when he looked at me and said, "Just stop it. Don't do it. It's not from God." Sure enough, he was right. When I looked at the list in 1st Corinthians, jealousy wasn't listed as one of the spiritual gifts.

Even with my jealousy under control, I hoped Lawler wouldn't regret our joining them as our new church family had no idea of the trouble my side of the family could bring with them to church. Most churchgoers had stories to tell about an incident that happened while they were rushing to get their families ready for Sunday school, or a funny story that happened during church hours. Ours had many!

Before I was born, our youngest brother Doug told the Sunday school teacher at the Methodist Church in Brady, Texas, that he wanted to sing a song called, "I got a hole in my bucket and I can't buy no beer," which he had heard on the jukebox just the day before.

Since my brothers shared the same Sunday school class and we were newcomers to the town, my older brother, Tommy, stated he was too embarrassed to ever go back to Sunday school. But Tommy got even with Doug.

On a spring day, Tommy needed to go home after Sunday school as his weakened hemophiliac body would not allow him to sit through church. Daddy carried him the few blocks to the house on his shoulders, with little Doug trailing along behind. Leaving the boys at the house, he reminded them of Momma's instructions to change immediately out of their church clothes. Doug was left in Tommy's care for just this one hour and Doug was told to help with whatever Tommy might need that wasn't already at his bedside.

Daddy walked back down the hill to church and since my sister Stella sat with a group of girls her own age and my parents were alone, they decided to abandon their back-pew habit and sit right up front by the preacher. My grandfather on my mother's side always reminded us that "Only sinners sit on the back pew," and I knew my Mother felt relieved to sit up front that Sunday.

The singing was finished and the preacher was deep into his sermon. Windows were open to let in the spring air and the congregation was fanning itself along with the rise and fall of the preacher's voice when the sobbing voice of a child was heard somewhere uphill from the church. The crying became louder and when it neared the front of the sanctuary, an usher arose from his post at the back of the church and stepped out of sight into the foyer. The crying proceeded to a higher wail as he apparently tried to restrain the child from entering the church.

The preacher stopped in mid-sermon. The congregation shifted in their seats, waiting as they would for a beautiful bride to enter the church doors, all eyes on the foyer door. The usher came slowly through the opening and down the long center aisle of the church. Beside him was my brother Doug, barefoot and clad in his oldest pair of pants with a dirty and torn shirt on wrong-side out. Doug was bawling loud enough to wake the dead and crying for our parents. Momma and Daddy sat frozen. Momma said she was both humiliated that the churchgoers were witnessing one of her sons in his dirtiest attire and frightened of what disaster Doug was going to relate. Sister Stella, being at a fragile age when everything embarrassed her, wanted to disappear into thin air and never come back to church again. This was before Doug even told his tale of woe.

Coming abreast of our parents' pew, Doug stopped crying and allowed himself to be passed from one churchgoer to the next until he was placed in his daddy's arms in the center of the pew. In his loudest voice, Doug said, "Tommy says he's dead, and I ain't staying in the house with a dead man!"

Only *my brothers* could embarrass a family so!

Last Sunday, my current family gathered to witness the baptism of our six-year-old grandson, Peyton. Sharla and six-month-old Abby were at home for a visit and along with Eddie, the four of us sat on a back pew instead of sitting up front with the rest of the family, fearful of any disturbance baby Abby might cause during the sermon or the baptism. The church family greeted and hugged each other and settled upon the pews facing the stained-glass windows at the head of the sanctuary. Under these sun-filled windows the preacher appeared in the baptismal tank and Peyton stepped out into the water. Prompted by Brother Troy Allen, Peyton bravely stated for all gathered to hear, "I accept Jesus as my Savior."

Supported by the preacher's strong hands, under the water his little body went, washing him clean for an easy entrance into heaven. Two pews of family at the front of the church swelled with pride at his proclamation and on the back pew, we cried silently, thanking God we were allowed to witness his baptism.

The war in Iraq was only a few days old and after Peyton's sins had been washed away, the preacher requested anyone having family in the military please stand and a special prayer would be said for them. Sharla proudly stood and all over the church, groups formed surrounding those who were standing in honor of their military family members. As a crowd gathered around us, I said, "This is my daughter, Sharla, and her husband Michael is overseas."

Fat-cheeked Abby, sleeping peacefully in her baby carrier on the pew, was a silent symbol of Michael and Sharla's love for each other.

A deacon prayed for Michael, for our family, and for the war to end quickly. As my chemotherapy was apparent by the absence of my eyebrows and eyelashes and because I wore a hat to mask my almost hairless head, those same worshipers included me in their prayers. Overwhelmed by the warmth I felt in this church, tears streamed down my cheeks and tasted salty on my tongue.

Eddie had handed me his handkerchief when Peyton was baptized and in the middle of this prayer for the military, Eddie needed the hanky worse than I did, as I could hear him sniffling loudly beside me. The prayer ended, hugs were exchanged, and warm smiles were handed out like sunshine after a rainstorm. Somehow I managed to curb my flow of tears.

Little Abby awoke halfway through the sermon and smiled her toothless way into my arms and my tears flowed again. I shook my head at how hard it had been for Sharla over the last six months, alone with a small sick baby so far away from home, plus continuously worrying about her mother and the safety of her husband. My thoughts turned to a day last July when my carefree life had come to a jolting halt and the long trail of surgery, hospital stays, chemo infusions, and the drastic alterations to my body had started. I thought about the horrible night Abby was born, gray and lifeless with the cord wrapped around her neck five times, and how I had bargained with God, on my knees on a cold hospital floor, to let her live. I had kept my end of the bargain to smile no matter what I had encountered during the last months and holding Abby in my arms was proof that God had kept his.

Forgetting I should be listening to the preacher, I insisted that God listen to me:

Look at me, Lord! You knew all along that I would be here watching our grandson get baptized and praying for Michael as a new war started overseas. Plus, you knew I would be holding this miracle of a granddaughter in my arms. Here I am—a survivor of breast cancer—sitting with other forgiven sinners on the back pew of the First Baptist Church in Florence, Texas. Exactly where you knew I would be today!

Inside the church, but thankfully only inside my head, I yelled,

"Lord, why can't we see where we are going? Why can't the blue of the sky become crystal clear and allow us to see where we are headed? It would have made my life so much easier if I could have seen this Sunday morning in March from my starting point last July."

I had to close my eyes to settle my emotions into an acceptable attitude for church.

When it was time to stand and sing the closing hymn, little Abby, who supposedly had hearing problems, joined right in and although the singing stopped between verses, Abby continued to praise the Lord in her own little monotone voice. She felt the music and the love in the church and followed the flow of the emotions in the air around her when she sang. The worshipers in the back pews turned and smiled as she praised the Lord.

It was time for the closing prayer. Eddie, to the right of me, placed his rough, work-worn hand in mine. Sharla, cradling Abby, managed to free one of her gentle mother's hands and slipped it into my left one for the final prayer. While I was feeling and comparing the vast differences between the texture of the skin, the shape and the size of their two hands in mine, Abby reached out and touched my face with her tiny sausage-shaped fingers. *Oh, the feeling of that tender hand upon my face!*

I opened my eyes and met her pair of sky-blue ones. Staring into her long-lashed eyes, I was reminded that I was looking at one of God's many miracles and I forgot all about being mad at the Lord only a few minutes before.

I didn't hear the prayer or its *Amen*. I stood and absorbed the feel of hands upon me as I thought about how many different kinds it took to make this Sunday. Preacher's strong hands, the pianist's hands, hands folded in prayers, hands that prepared Sunday dinner. Hard, work-worn hands, gentle hands, innocent hands, and most of all, God's loving hands.

"Sinners Row" was a great place to be that Sunday.

My mother and dad would have surely rather had my Sunday experience than the one involving Doug's request for a beer song and Tommy's portrayal of a dead man, but another Sunday morning made up for all the embarrassing moments at church they had with us as children.

One Easter when all four of us kids were grown, we gathered at home for the holiday and as usual, Mother's wish for any occasion was that we all attend church together. We helped get lunch started, dressed in our Easter best, and went to church, all except for Tommy who was too weak to join us.

At the crowded church service, we had to sit two rows from the front on one long pew. The services started and while announcements were being made, the congregation behind us became uncommonly quiet and the preacher gazed up the aisle toward the church doors. We turned in our seats to look behind us.

No, not a bride and not Doug in his dirty clothes. Tommy, with his crippled leg and because of his refusal to use his crutches, was making his way slowly and painfully down the aisle to where we sat. With the helpful hand of God and without the family hovering over his every move, he had gotten dressed and driven himself to what would be his last Easter Sunday church service on this earth.

As he forced his weak body to walk down to the front of the church, he was surely silently discussing with Grandfather the phrase engrained in our minds at an early age: "Each time you walk into a church, always sit up front, close to the preacher."

My parents forgave Tommy for pulling his dead-man trick on Doug long before, but that special Sunday is a treasured part of my life and I thank God for allowing me to witness another spring of Sundays here with my family.

I pray that I will have many more days on earth to join our family in church. After all, who knows what could happen on the back row of church next Sunday?

Who may ascend the hill of the Lord? Who may stand in his holy place? He who has clean hands and a pure heart.

—Psalm 24:3

Chapter 19

Closet Secrets

"Life must be understood backwards; but it must be lived forward.
                    Soren Kierkeguard

The closet was full of the smells of old leather shoes and mothballs as the Great Aunts hardly ever opened the door and aired it. Light came in from around the old wooden door and reflected off the white of the porcelain doorknob and I noticed it shinning more and more as my eyes became accustomed to the dark. Enclosed together in the semi-darkness, Doug had me spit in the palm of my hand and swear to secrecy that I would never tell another "living soul" about what he was going to whisper in my ear.

Since I hadn't been introduced to any "dead souls" that I could think of to share his many secrets with, I knew better than to open my mouth and tell anyone about his tales of mischief. Doug reminded me often that the punishment for breaking our secret pack would be self-inflicted. He said my long blonde locks would immediately start to fall out and I would be bald in less than an hour. He informed me that this was the reason I saw so many baldheaded men, as everyone knew a grown man couldn't keep a secret!

Doug's secret today involved a love note from a boy that he had discovered while snooping in Stella's dresser. Oh, would she be mad! Maybe this one time I should tell on him so she could put a stop to Doug's invasion of her privacy! But I thought again of all the bald-headed men we sat behind at church whose heads shined like porcelain doorknobs reflecting the sanctuary lights, and I stood fast and let Doug finish his tale.

Standing in that closet I was the perfect height to feel the button cuffs, as they would brush across my face when I buried myself deep between the garments. I must have been no older than four or five, which means I kept Doug's closet secrets to myself for over four decades. Now, since I had actually experienced baldness, which as you know was not related to the disclosure of any secrets, I felt I had every right to purge myself of his secret entreaties. Problem is, I couldn't remember the ones that amounted to anything worth telling! Possibly, they never did.

So, I had it my head that I should be allowed to tell another secret that I carried around with me for months, one that I *did* remember, as a reward for being totally bald those four months. I struggled with myself, weighing the pros and cons of "telling" and especially putting it in writing where it could never be erased or forgotten, but I deserved to share my secret with my friends.

Our older brother Tommy had hemophilia. Tommy spent his entire life hemorrhaging in one or more places in his body at any given time. Hemophilia is not the type of disease you get to take chemo or radiation as a treatment and pray it stays away afterward. You live, eat, and breathe off the constant blood transfusions and you are in constant pain from the bruising. He doubled his life expectancy only because he had his mind set on living and never allowed himself to give up until he decided nothing was left except for his constant companion of pain.

Stella was the oldest, then Tommy, then Doug, and then me. Boys get the disease, girls don't, but they pass on the gene. Since Doug didn't have hemophilia, he was safe. Stella had a girl named Debbie and a healthy boy named Billy. Debbie had two healthy boys and one girl. That one girl, my great niece, was the only possible link to hemophilia that our family could pass on, except by me, but at an early age I made up my mind never to bear children. I opted not to take a chance of bringing another hemophiliac child into this world and although I kept all the right parts until I was forty-eight, with God's grace, I managed to prevent any pregnancy.

In my young married years, I often prayed for a test that could tell me positively that I carried, or better yet, did not carry, the hemophilia gene as the medical books had only case histories to base statistics on and they listed my odds as twelve to one the baby would be born with the disease. Today, the comparison of Tommy's DNA and mine or my nieces would tell the truth and up until just lately, I had always thought I needed to know. So, if it were necessary, I could apologize to God for making the wrong decision.

Did I take the right path or the wrong one? Did I hold back on God? Did I not use my body as he intended for me to do when he made me a girl? I was afraid my decision to be childless was just that—my decision, not God's—and I spent many a fretful night wondering if I prevented a child from being born that God intended to walk on this earth.

The hemophilia foundation, seeking to stop the dreaded disease, found me a precious three-day-old baby to call my own and I spent my life concerned for Sharla Beth's well being, just as any mother would for a child she birthed. I hoped to have always treated her as the gift she was from God and, I believed she would say she never lacked for a mother's love. Sharla coming into my life filled my need to nurture.

On the other hand, until much later in her life, I did not provide Sharla with a good father and before the ink was dry on the adoption papers, her adoptive father asked me for a divorce and in less than thirty days he had married a woman who presented him with a son in less than a year. He took most of my heart with him and then unknowingly stabbed what was left of it with a very sharp knife when his son was born. All this pain taught me a lesson I never forgot: it would be a rare man indeed who did not need his own children to verify his manhood.

When my heart finally sealed its wound, I looked for children who needed a mother and soon found two little blonde-headed boys, Kevin and Mark, older than Sharla, and promptly married their father. After these two boys were raised, I moved on and considered myself lucky to find a man who had two daughters, ReGina and Rissa, both older than Sharla, and we married. Today each of the five children God blessed me with is married and has two children of their own. Added to this "Brady Bunch" was two of Eddie's young cousins and along with their spouses and their two children, we never lacked for company on the holidays. My houseful of children and grandchildren are all heaven sent and I have received more blessings than I deserve and am quite content with my family and my sweet husband.

What about the secret? Well, back in time, when my heart was broken and my blood was still fresh upon the ground, a young man fell in love with little Sharla and then me. He was a good man and offered us a life with him, but I refused. I could not allow him to marry us when a chance existed he would never be satisfied with just Sharla. I knew his family counted on him to carry on the family name and I stood firm and ended our relationship one foggy eve. As I drove away from where he was leaning up against his pickup on that dark night, the fog made him appear to evaporate before my very eyes. And evaporate he did; for twenty-five years we neither saw nor spoke to each other again.

This man received word that I was sick and surprised me with a phone call. Only after our long conversation could I finally put to rest my old question of whether I had gone against God's will when I refused to give life to a child. For this young man who had evaporated from my life so many years ago married another, moved to the tip of Texas, and fathered five healthy boys and five healthy girls! If I had never become ill, I doubt I would have ever known about his fabulous family.

Nearly everybody has a secret love or lost boyfriend in her past so the telling of this story is not really too spectacular. Unless I add a postscript. Step deeper into the dark closet with me and let your eyes grow accustom to the dark and I'll whisper in your ear something I probably shouldn't tell. But first you have to spit in your hand and swear to never tell another living soul. Okay? Ready?

One of this man's daughters is now a part of our company's staff. Every working day I am allowed to see her beautiful face and I listen for her footsteps in the corridor outside my office door, light steps that remind me of how lucky I am. Besides the children and the grandchildren I cherish within my household, God has allowed me the opportunity to meet first-hand an indirect product of a heavy-hearted decision I made a long time ago: a living product, which along with her brothers and sisters blesses another household. Someday soon when I get to know her better I'll have to tell her this story. Until then, remember, you promised to keep my secret!

Let everything that has breath praise the Lord.
PSALM 150:6

Chapter 20

Perfect Center

A piece of the miracle process has been reserved for each of us.
— Jim Rohn

Two masked doctors stitched on the flesh of my chest today and produced a likeness of the two old friends I used to see when I gazed into my bathroom mirror. Now, even though my newly made buttons were covered in gauze, I could already feel the depth and the new dimension the buttons added to my previously blank chest. I wanted to rip off their protective coverings and ignore the soreness of the just-completed surgery and flash my image in the bathroom mirror that along with me must wait impatiently for the day of unveiling to arrive.

As I lay on that operating table, I was allowed to move only my eyes and was urged to keep perfectly still. I was too scared at first to watch their hands as they manipulated my flesh and I used the backsides of my eyelids as tiny screens and viewed the sweet faces of all my grandchildren, faces captured on a mind video labeled "Love" that during the last year and a half, I kept stored within easy reach for such occasions as this. I listened to the laughter of the children and the sound of their voices and used both to mask the doctor's instructions to his staff, as I truly did not need to understand any of their comments until one would announce they had completed their work of art.

During the second half-hour of forced immobility, I opened my eyes and watched the faces of the two plastic surgeons. Their concentration was astounding! Why would they take time to perfect the chest of some big-a-round woman like me? Why all the measuring and marking to find the perfect center to do their magic? Why not just give it your best guess and install the flesh where you think it should go and save your perfection for a pretty, young woman who could display your handiwork in crowded rooms of admirers and advertise your skills as she reverently spoke your name. Why would these two doctors waste their talents on a lady too big to turn a man's head and too old to press a baby to her breast?

As their graceful hands fastidiously sewed flesh-to-flesh, I marveled at the buds of tissue they were sculpturing just for me. When these healed, I would be ready for tattoos. Tears formed as I thought about the women diagnosed with breast-cancer who would never make it to this final operating room and would be laid to rest breathless, and breastless, at the end of their own cancer walks. Would God's first blessing to them when they arrived at his pearly gates be to grant them a second set of perfectly formed breasts along with their glistening wings?

With such thoughts gathering in my head, my lids could not hold my tears and I was glad the doctors were busy with their work and did not notice the water slip from beneath my newly grown-in-again eyelashes and run slowly down the sides of my face, mascara outlining the trail. The urge to reach up and brush the tears away was almost overpowering; yet, I managed to keep my arms down by my sides. I lay in my pool of tears and thanked God I was allowed to experience the pain and the passion of reconstruction surgery.

I no longer asked, "Why me, Lord," with anger in my voice as I did when first informed of my breast cancer. I had been humbled by the love from my friends and family, the kindness displayed to me from perfect strangers as they stood behind me and my bald head at the grocery store, and the skills of the many doctors and technicians who treated my body as if it were that of a beautiful teenage girl who had yet to have her first date.

I now asked in disbelief, in a voice filled with awe, "Why me, Lord?"

> *When the crowd saw this, they were filled with awe; and they praised God, who had given such authority to men.*
>
> MATTHEW 9:8

Chapter 21

Wanted: One Baby Gorilla

Laughter dulls the sharpest pain and flattens out the greatest stress. To share it is to give a gift of health.
                                               BARBARA JOHNSON

Being able to laugh at myself played a large part in my healing process. Just before my nipple reconstruction surgery, Stella and I had taken a Survivor Cruise and I had joked about the topless, topless deck, where women like me could remove our bathing suit tops and get a suntan. After all, we breastless women still enjoyed the feel of hot sun on bare skin, although for the most part, my new chest had no feeling. Stella, always afraid her little sister would embarrass her again, had made me hush when I brought it up the second time. She explained it was okay for me to joke about it, but it was in poor taste for her to laugh about it. I disagreed, but snickered to myself about my quip for the rest of the cruise. Aggravating her further, I placed Halloween stick-on spider webs where my nipples should have been, making sure my bathing suit top was pulled down low enough so the edges of the webs were visible. Needless to say, she wasn't happy with my idea of spider web tattoos!

Another funny thing happened, completely unexpected. I thought my two mounds had looked odd without nipples; now though, as I stared into the bathroom mirror, I was horrified with my new ones. Maybe I should have waited a couple more days before changing the bandages. The two perfectly sculptured forms of two-days ago, now protruded a good three-quarters of an inch and measured a half-an-inch wide! I could have easily nursed a baby gorilla! Lord, what were the doctors thinking of when they stitched these on for me?

Shaking my head in disbelief, I backed away from the mirror and sat heavily on the commode lid. Where would I find a bra with enough padding to corral them so they wouldn't tent my blouses? It would take a strip of silver duct tape to keep them semi-flat. Tattoos around these things would be as large as Saturn's rings! Maybe I should have kept my two blanks.

The doctor had said not to sleep lying on my stomach because I would squash them. That was a laugh! It would take a ten-pound rock with a fifty-pound gorilla standing on top to level these babies! Imagining myself lying flat with a rock on each breast and a gorilla jumping up and down on each rock, made me laugh. Once the laughter started, I couldn't stop. Staggering out of the bathroom, I met Eddie coming to see what was so funny.

"Have you seen any gorillas hanging around the ranch lately? I think we're going to need one or two," I managed to say through my laughter.

Afraid he had heard me correctly, and not wanting to pursue the remark any further, he didn't even stop. Rolling his eyes, he headed out the back door. I doubted he was going to look for gorillas in the pecan trees out back. More than likely, he would find a quiet place to call on the Lord, asking help in retaining his sanity, as it appeared, once again, that I had lost mine.

Taking one more quick peek at the enormous nipples, I covered them with clean gauze and buttoned my blouse. I made a date for knee-mail that night as soon as Eddie was asleep and the house was quiet. Surely God didn't intend for me to brag on his handiwork while wearing a two-inch pad of gauze secured by a piece of duct tape? Thank goodness I didn't really have any milk to secrete through my "Milk Duds," as one of my friends had laughingly described them, or the front of my shirt would never have been dry.

Thankfully, the nipples shrank in size. In December the incisions were not yet healed, so I couldn't take the last step in my reconstruction project. I had wanted to send out Christmas cards that said, "All I want for Christmas is my two tattoos," but my family wouldn't go along with my idea. I spent the next few weeks wondering if I could ask for tattoos of the pink breast cancer survivor ribbon or maybe, better yet, two bull's eyes or two happy faces. Stella wouldn't even joke with me about it!

In January I bared my breasts and watched as a no-nonsense clinician tattooed on the areola, the brown ring around my nipples. She dipped the end of what resembled a wood-burning tool into a color mixed especially for my skin tone. Stepping on a floor pedal, she made seven very sharp little needles stick their heads out and gored the flesh surrounding the newly made nipple. When she paused for more color, I opened my eyes and looked down at my chest just in time to see blood spurt from the latest seven little holes. She injected numbing medicine near my cleavage where I still have a few intact nerve endings, but it was still painful in those areas. Who in their right mind would ever endure the pain of getting a tattoo?

Later, when the bandages came off, I was quite pleased with the outcome and extremely proud of my new chest! I had discovered something wonderful after the implants were installed; I could cross my arms under my breasts and feel the weight of them resting on my arms, another "womanly" feeling I thought I had lost. The only other odd thing I encountered (besides searching for the correct area to shave and apply deodorant) is when I pledge allegiance to our American flag; I can't feel my hand across my chest. I assume I will eventually get used to the lack of any feeling from shoulder to shoulder but isn't it funny how much of God's miraculous construction of the human body we take for granted until it is gone.

The last two steps in reconstruction of my chest were finished. All that was left was the removal of my port. I watched the overhead monitor as the line running straight into a main artery was removed. My Titanium friend, which had made access to my body easy for nearly two years, was gone. Now I would have to take blood tests, shots, and IVs the old, painful, way. I would also have to break my habit of feeling for the security of it, nestled inside my arm. Yet, without its constant reminder that at one time I needed it for chemo infusions, I really started to feel like a survivor.

It was time to let my scars heal and move on. I typed a chapter and mailed it with a cover letter stating I was near the end of the breast-cancer series. Little did I know, I could write epilogue after epilogue to this never-ending story as a completed battle of any kind leaves the door wide open for at least one more chapter. I'm happy to say, God wasn't through with me yet.

> *Our mouths were filled with laughter, our tongues with songs of joy. The Lord has done great things for us, and we are filled with joy.*
>
> Psalms 126: 2, 3

Chapter 22

A Time to Dance

How vain it is to sit down to write when you have not stood up to live.
HENRY DAVID THOREAU 1817-1862

I had been feeling so fit this last year, settling down was hard for me, especially when the birds were singing and the sun shined brightly in the east window beside my computer, both beckoning me outside. I told myself God would let me know when the time was right to record the last chapter of my cancer walk, and today, a breezy Saturday in April, He nudged my heart by sending two old friends to tell me.

At lunchtime when I finished the first draft of a Mother's Day tribute, I managed to quickly make a tuna salad and exchange my dirty shirt for a clean one, all in an effort to make my 1:30 beauty shop appointment. Throwing plates on the table, I glanced out the kitchen window and saw something I hadn't seen this close to the house before. A lone dove was sitting in the high grass under the fence directly in front of the table. She was sitting perfectly still, adorned with a coat of light brown feathers, fully at ease and not the least bit nervous that four old tomcats guard my house and the grounds surrounding it. I pointed out the dove to the family and although I thought I never took my eyes off of her, she was suddenly gone. I hastily ate my sandwich and as I left for the beauty shop, wondered why a dove would be so close to the house.

I felt very much at home at my beauty shop. Beauticians, who knew me when I had long auburn hair and had missed me the year I was bald, joyfully welcomed me back when the peach fuzz began to appear. Now, almost a year since the first new sprouts of hair adorned my head, Jere, my hairdresser at *New Reflections*, put a towel around my neck and I felt something that I thought I would never feel again. He took his left hand and lifted my hair off the back of my neck! Hair so thick and heavy that I had already become accustomed to its new weight on a neck that had felt the chill of every wind just a short winter ago.

Tears ran down my face. Seeing the raw emotion spilling down the front of my cape and trying to understand what had caused my outburst of tears, my friends gathered beside me. We recognized that I had come full circle from where I had started when the cancer appeared and led me down a path on which no one ever wished to wander. When I announced my breast cancer and that I was afraid of losing not only a breast but also upset over losing my hair, Jere had stated I would be back again for my monthly haircut. It was great to hear him say, "I told you so!"

Regretting that I had caused tears to be shed, and in keeping with my mission of spreading the news about how early detection can help women survive breast cancer, I told a couple of the new patrons how God had not only given me this new head of thick and curly hair, but how He had also provided me with a new manmade chest. I explained that I had allowed a plastic surgeon to completely rebuild my chest. True, I had lost only one breast to cancer in the beginning, but made a tough decision the day before my reconstruction surgery and asked that the other one be removed too. Medically, I probably made the right decision, but it was a tough one as with both breasts gone, I would never again experience the feel of a rough hand cupping my breast, or feel lips upon my nipples.

I explained my lightening-quick, second mastectomy, two implants, and intensive liposuction procedures. I stressed the important part: I was up and active on the fourth day and proud of my new breasts although they were so high the first few weeks, I felt as if I would smother and needed extra face powder to cover them! But, in just a few short weeks the swelling went down and I again had cleavage and two matching breasts.

I informed all the ladies that the best part about the implants being built-in behind my chest muscles was that I would never have to wear a bra again. I told them that the biggest problem I encountered after the surgery was that my armpits were now further down my sides and I had to shave hair off my rib cage! The procedure came with a ten-year deflation warranty on the two implants and I laughingly told everyone ten years *or* 10,000 hugs, whichever comes first!

I told my audience that the nipple construction was miraculous! I watched the entire procedure from flat on my back as the plastic surgeon made a quick incision on each new breast, pulled the skin down and around, and formed two round mounds of flesh creating me a pair of nipples! I had come a long way from the girl who had fainted just stepping into the doorway of a hospital to the woman mesmerized by the doctor's attempt to make her feel whole again.

They laughed with me when I said that two nights later in front of my mirror, I got the fright of my life when I took off the dressings. The new nipples were big enough to nurse baby gorillas and I almost let myself cry at the sight of them! I asked God to *please* let mine shrink to at least nickel size, which they did in just a few short days.

I got my point across to the ladies at the beauty shop that losing your hair and your breasts does not cause you to lose yourself. I was the same as before, only now more appreciative of God's gifts, like the weight of my hair and my new breasts. I looked for signs of God's love and often stopped to smell the flowers I once would have overlooked. For example, this spring, thousands of women lined the San Antonio River Walk after a Woman's Faith convention and I seemed to be the only one who stopped and smelled the lovely scent of the wisteria blooms climbing on the rock walls.

Halfway through my story at the beauty shop, I realized that God had sent me the quiet dove that morning to remind me that I had traveled full circle from the beginning of my cancer journey to the place I am today. I am finished with all my surgeries, wearing a headful of thick curly hair, and displaying my new chest covered with a purple "Relay for Life" tee shirt that proudly states "Survivor" on the back.

I finished my story by urging the women to schedule an annual mammogram and then something familiar about one of the customers having her hair done kept nagging at me. I asked the lady, "Do I seem familiar to you?"

Comparing our places of employment all the way back to our first real jobs, we realized we had been friends thirty-four years before!

I came home that afternoon full of news of her family and looked through an old photograph album covered in closet dust. Among other pictures of my youth was one of Margaret and me in our bathing suits, both of us proudly parading our young breasts. I admit while staring at the picture, I once again cried for the loss of my breasts, but quickly reminded myself to be thankful for my new pair and for the reunion with my friend.

Now when I removed my blouse at night and saw my new breasts and the fading scars that adorn my body like twining leafless vines, I thought of the Bible verse:

> *"There is a time for everything, and a season for every activity under heaven...a time to weep and a time to laugh, a time to mourn, a time to dance..."*
>
> ECCLESIASTES 3:1, 4 NIV.

CHAPTER 23

Life's Sweet Frosting

*Each day comes bearing its own gifts.
Untie the ribbons.*
                    RUTH ANN SCHABACKER

Fingerprints from tiny hands adorned my low kitchen windows and tiny kisses for the tomcats were smeared across the back glass door, sweet kisses meant for cats a mere thin pane away from a chubby toddler's grasp. Red Popsicle marked the spot where laughter and sweet syrup burst from her mouth as she rode happily along in the car headed for her first visit to a Texas beach. A bright orange swing with bright blue ropes swung empty of a rider, clashing with the yellow siding and brown trim of the ranch house. All of these were signs that a sweet little miracle named Abigail was here.

Temporary necessities used to occupy her time with us would soon disappear from sight. The swimming pool had already lost its air and hung limply across a picnic table, and like the wooden high chair speckled with her breakfast oatmeal, must be scrubbed and put away to wait for her return another day. Borrowed toys from a sweet grandmother down the road, who knew the expense to entertain a small child, were boxed and ready to be returned. They looked forlorn, sitting idly in the garage, bored without the life her little fingers gave them and perfectly quiet without the sound of her sweet little voice singing along to their music. I envied the car seat that accompanied her on the plane ride to her Tennessee grandmother's house, and wished they could have shipped me instead, as my now healthy body made of flesh and bones would have gladly held her tightly if only I had been allowed.

Already my few evenings after work seem empty without her greeting me at the door with her frantic cries of "out tide, out tide." Silly me, I was afraid before she came to visit that she might not know Granny Pat, as I had only been able to see her a few times in her twenty months of life, and the last time she was here, I was bald. But I quickly discovered she would always be my companion no matter how I looked if I helped her open the back door and escape into the outside world. She was truly mine for a month that turned out to be the second wettest June we can remember and we enjoyed hopping after the crop of tiny, springy, freshly hatched frogs and trailing after a slow-moving turtle making its way from one stock tank to another.

She stood under miniature waterfalls just her size on the backside of the tank dam and learned the joy of dropping rocks into puddles to make a splash that could reach all the way to your face, if the rock was big enough. We would come inside muddy and wet and needing a bubble bath to make us all clean again and her momma would shake her head and wonder out loud, "Just what in world am I going to do to keep Abigail entertained back home in our little house in the middle of a big military base?"

I missed our nighttime ritual of buckling up Abigail, her momma, and Granny Mac in the "Mule" and racing like fast car drivers across the pastures, waving at cows and chasing jackrabbits on our way to visit Uncle Troy and Aunt Rene. Or better yet, finding Aunt Rissa and Uncle Stacy at home and having the opportunity to watch her hug her cousins, Peyton, Lyndzey, Tyler, and Chandler and repeat phrases they had taught her such as, "What's up, Dude?" and watch her point her index fingers in the air and "disco" to music only she could hear. All the time, I was thanking God that I finished my battle with breast cancer and was quite able to join her in a dance to the make-believe music.

She quickly discovered in which pasture the cows could be found and her "moos" would fill the air long before the first cow could be sighted. Touching one of the ranch dogs was pure joy to Abby and we should reward the Great Pyrenees for allowing Abby to rest her little body up against his thick coat of white hair, and we should thank the Corgi for not biting her when she escalated the shedding of his coat by pulling out handfuls of his soft red hair. Forget the cats, as they were never Abby's friends no matter how many times she chased them through the yard and up a tree, repeating her rendition of "meow." Thinking all the while that she could communicate to them either in words or in sign language how very much she wanted to feel their soft fur and touch their elusive whiskers.

It didn't matter to the birds in the trees that Abigail had severe hearing loss in one ear and moderate loss in the other; they sang her a song anyway, every time she managed to escape from the house and run barefoot up the long caliche drive toward the cows in the hayfield. The newly installed electric gate was dubbed "Abby's gate" as we found we must keep it closed to provide protection for the cows from the ever curious child and we took turns retrieving her from that gate. The ranch was never as lively as when she was here and the ranch hands were never quite as tired or as sore at night after a day of chasing the runaway and hauling her "pig style" under their arms back to the safety of the house. Three days after she left, my hip joints had finally quit hurting, but my heart felt it would never heal. When my tears threatened to fall because I missed her so badly, I reminded myself that just twelve months ago the soreness of my chest after reconstruction would not have allowed me to hold her, and just look at me now! How well I knew what time and prayer could heal.

While she was here, we entered her in the town's annual baby contest and although they did not draw her name from the fishbowl and proclaim her the winner, she entertained the crowd and got the most applause from her antics. She rode proudly in the lap of her mother on my company's float in the Florence Friendship Day parade and their picture appeared on the front page of our little town newspaper. Guess who bought a dozen copies?

I missed her sky-blue eyes, her Shirley Temple golden curls, and her pug nose. She was the spitting image of her mother at that age and I would always consider her a lifetime gift from Sharla to me. Along with our other children and their families, Abigail seemed like life's sweet frosting on an already delicious cake.

The sweetest video I filmed of Abigail was one my family would always cherish. Granny Mac at eighty-three and little Abigail holding hands and moving to the loud volume of the children's music playing on some old LP records Mother put on every night for Abigail's enjoyment. The oldest and the youngest of my family sharing a precious segment that none of us would ever be able to capture again. Abby would be much older the next time she came to visit and Mother had a harder time moving about every day. Many times this last month I said how much I would like to freeze this place in time as those I loved most dearly were safe and warm and nearby and I was cancer free. I found that sweet times such as this didn't happen often in life and I would never take happiness for granted again after my walk down the breast-cancer pathway.

Miss Independent was Sharla's and now Abby's nickname. The two of them should have been born on the 4th of July, as both liked to make their own decisions. Poor little Abby stayed in trouble a lot during her visit and I think toward the end of the month, Sharla began to think that I might have had something to do with it. Abby and I did finally manage to convince her mother that in some instances "No" was appropriate and that Abby should not be scolded for using the forbidden word when her Granny Pat was the one who was aggravating her. Sometimes a child needed to lay down the law when grandmothers stole too much sugar or worse yet, when grandmothers tried to slip out the back door without you. Shame, shame, shame!

I should be shot for teaching Abby to say, "I'm mean," and after receiving threats from Granny Mac, I did teach her to say "I'm sweet,": both spoken with the longest Texan drawl she could manage. We progressed to the word "terrible" only Abby said "tarable" and we used the word to describe stinky britches and enforced bedtimes and finally, we used that one and only word to express our feelings when Sharla took her from my arms and they walked through the security checkpoint at the airport. It was a "tarable" "tarable" "tarable" time for all three of us but I kept remembering the last time they left from the airport. I was bald and so completely worn out from their short visit and the chemo treatments that my sweet husband had to hold me tight to keep me from collapsing. This time at their departure, I drove us to the airport, carried luggage into the terminal, and chased Abigail until time for her to go. There was no sign of the sick and disheveled woman from just a few months ago.

I kept reminding myself that her daddy, Michael, was protecting our country by training soldiers at Fort Jackson in South Carolina and that we must all be strong and brave and consider our lost time together as our sacrifice for peace. Yet, somehow, I couldn't convince myself that the loss of the feeling of her soft baby arms wrapped around my neck had anything to do with guns, or raging wars, or freedom.

I wouldn't forget the feel of her pink sticky skin pressed tightly against my body as she lay her head upon my shoulder and we slowly rocked ourselves into a quieter place to sleep the night away. Her sweet baby smell after her bath each night would remain the only fragrance I wished to wear for a long time to come and I was thinking of wearing baby lotion on my body to the office to see if it could work its soothing magic on those I encountered each day.

If I could fit into her baby bed that I left standing for a few more days, I would curl up under the yellow blanket that she and her mother before her slept under, and spend a night sleeping and dreaming of the sweet things she carried with her when she closed her eyes at night. I would like to think that her dreams at night in Tennessee or back home in South Carolina would contain a few scenes that include her grandmothers and the rest of her Texas family.

She left us on a big Delta plane and arrived safely to the awaiting arms of Michael's parents, her half-sister Leah, and best of all, her dad. I was told that she repeated all her new words and phrases and then ended her performance with a phrase she might use every time she found herself in trouble. She discovered that it worked well when her grandmother wound her up too tight and her momma had to speak sternly to the little darling. Her little face would gaze up into yours with its blue, blue eyes and pug nose and say, "Nanny did it!" If it could save her some spankings, I hoped she never forgot that phrase.

I heard she called for her "Nanny" when Sharla put her to bed the first night and I heard her crying the second night over the phone. (I bet she was upset that she was not going to have a nightly ride to see the cows.) I hadn't heard tonight how she fared when they put her to bed nor had anyone in the family here thought to ask how I was doing. If they bothered to check on me, I'd say my heart was heavy and my green eyes were very full of tears. If pressed to state the reason for my sadness, I would have to admit: "Abby did it!"

My knees were good for knee-mail to our Lord and at times like this I sought a quiet place (with carpet for good padding) and thanked Him for keeping His end of the bargain and letting Sharla have her baby. Yes, I know He had her little life planned before she was ever conceived, but her living and growing into such a beautiful toddler made me feel that God was pleased enough with me in my fight with the breast cancer to allow Abigail Patricia Williams the chance to know her grandmother. The two of us were miracles as we walked here today, both marvels of medical science conducted under the watchful guidance of our Lord. Me with my two manmade breasts and she with her two little hearing aids.

My love for those around me multiplied and I felt more empathy for others than ever. I understood the fear of being told you have cancer, understood the fear of becoming someone else after a surgeon altered your body forever, but I could also hold another woman's hand who had just been diagnosed with cancer and truthfully tell her that her life was going to change in ways she could never believe, most of which would be for the better. Just ask my sweet husband how much our lives changed.

He wouldn't tell you that our bedroom experiences were any different from how they used to be because of the changes in my body, because they weren't, but he would tell you how unnerved he was when I surprised him and everybody else by becoming friends with his ex-wife after sixteen years of trying to establish my place in his family's hearts. Besides making a grand effort to treat her as a sister in Christ and put all jealousy aside, I found out when I had cancer just who loved me and how much they really cared. Room existed for both of us and I no longer felt crowded by her presence. I should have a T-shirt made with that old advertisement slogan that said, "You've come along way, Babe," and wear it proudly along with my now shoulder-length hair and parade around our little town.

I was in love with living and although I still would like to stay curled up tight in my bed in the mornings all cozy and comfortable as I was before my first surgery, I strove to have me and my smile to work on time every morning. After all, miracles were performed that allowed me to keep my job and I knew when I got there that I was surrounded by employees who fought and prayed with me during my cancer battle and the battle to keep that job. I lived not only inside of God's protective arms but also protected in a community that knew the difference between right and wrong. My battle with breast cancer brought out the best in a lot of us.

Abigail's parents would hopefully be stationed closer to home before she got too much older and she and I would strengthen our bond and my little pack of grandchildren would be complete. I continued to help other women through their ordeal with breast cancer until another way to walk the cancer path can be found. "Knee-mail" continues to be our biggest hope that someday, hopefully in the near future, a woman faced with breast cancer wouldn't have to go through what I and many others before me had to endure. To think that any woman should have to undertake such a life-changing ordeal was still overwhelming.

Looking toward the future, now I had a passion for life and for writing that would never have come to the forefront had I not witnessed firsthand my very real drama of surviving breast cancer and its subsequent treatments. I intended to continue to listen to God and allow Him to guide my fingers as I sat each night at my keyboard. And if anyone asked how I managed to make it through my battle and come out on the other end with more strength than when I started, I would truthfully have to say, "God did it."

You turned my wailing into dancing: you removed my sackcloth and clothed me with joy, that my heart may sing to you and not be silent. O Lord my God, I will give you thanks forever.

Psalms 30:11, 12

Chapter 24

Stepping Out

> *None of us will ever accomplish anything excellent or commanding except when he listens to this whisper which is heard by him alone.*
> RALPH WALDO EMERSON

Months went by before I realized I had changed. There was no other way to justify the "fish out of water" feeling I had each day at work. Patty Cakes, the child who continuously sought gratification from her peers, would have raced to erase any traces of the doubts Daemon described to the Board of Directors concerning her job performance. The new Patty recognized that the only one she needed to please was the one who furnished the doctors with their talent to create her pretty pink chest. I was not afraid to admit that I had doubts concerning my abilities to guide the fast-growing company. Was I standing in the way with my limited education in the business field? Was my discontent because I felt God had something else in mind for me to do?

What about the book I had started writing? If completed, could it be of help to another woman facing breast cancer or one attempting to help her sister through her ordeal? My mailing list of ladies, waiting for me to send the latest chapter, had reached the one-hundred mark and was still growing, leading me to believe I was at least entertaining with my stories. The four-part skit I had written from the chapter entitled, "Snip, Snip," had been a success at the latest cancer retreat and I had been asked to present it again. Friends of friends sought my advice, or gave me a phone number of a woman seeking a confident voice to talk to about her fears, while struggling to make life-altering choices concerning her own body. How could I be of help, Lord? Shouldn't I be spreading the word about how early detection saved my life? Where was my broadcasting platform?

I hadn't spent that much time worrying over my future since I had pondered the boy-girl question before my tenth birthday. I felt like a tightly wound spool of thread awaiting the push of the sewing machine's pedal. Unrolling wouldn't take long once the seamstress got started. I had the feeling that something short of a burning bush was going to reveal itself and give me the push I needed to step out and start anew. Luckily, I was paying attention when my premonition came true.

Eddie owned a car wash in the middle of our little town of Florence. A fine car wash with three bays and even a cycle of "spot free rinse." Lots of people used his car wash and bragged on it because he kept it as clean as the dairy he was raised on. Like clockwork he got up two hours before dawn and drove into Florence where he hosed down the bays with hot water before customers arrived.

One "perk" to owning a car wash besides making a quarter or two off of every wash was that you got to pick up all the odds and ends that customers accidentally left behind. I try not to get too excited when Eddie came home with a new find because honestly, most of it was simply wet junk. But each week he found two or three of the magnetic ribbons that get blown off cars when their owners wash them with the high-pressure wash. Eddie brought them home and stuck them on the spare refrigerator in the garage and I distributed them to needy cars. Today, our inventory held six different "supports" in six different colors of ribbons.

On my personal van I had a yellow "Support Your Troops" magnet in honor of Michael, and to show my respect to the other soldiers I came into contact with around Ft Hood. I also had the only pink magnetic ribbon I had ever seen with the word "Survivor" printed across it. When I found the one and only "Survivor" ribbon, the lady selling it said it was a sample and apparently neither she nor anyone else around here ever ordered any.

Both ribbons meant a lot to me but the pink one pointed out to anyone behind my car that I was a breast-cancer survivor! A title I proudly wore!

With all my traveling around and because breast cancer is prevalent, I knew I must sit at a stoplight once in a while where a woman in a car behind me would be encouraged by reading my declaration. My tailgate friend might have just had a bad biopsy and be facing more tests or possibly she just received a letter telling her to come back for a repeat mammogram. Knowing other women survived the ordeal of breast cancer was always important to me when I started my battle and I felt the need to share my victory with other women starting theirs.

Anyway, I was very proud of my pink magnet and also very protective of it. At the airport or other major parking lots, I removed it and placed it inside the car. Surely no one would stoop so low as to steal my pink one, but I didn't want to take a chance. Eddie had never found one like it floating in the muddy water at the car wash so I felt it was very rare. Plus, when the nation moved onto another fad and the pink ribbon needed to be retired, I planned on placing it in the antique trunk along with the articles left there for me by my ancestors. I wanted my descendants to know how proud I was to be a survivor.

So, anyway, I don't mind washing my car at Eddie's clean car wash, but you ladies know what a chore it is to get out of your car and wash it the old-fashioned way. I liked to run it through a laser car wash. One where you could stay seated and let the car wash do the work. Sometimes when heading to Killeen or Georgetown, I asked Eddie for a few of his newest dollar bills to feed into the touchy collection slot at the laser car wash. (Eddie probably thought I gave them to the grandchildren for the collection plate at church.) If no one was at the laser-wash facility who could witness the owner's wife of the Florence car wash washing her car at another facility, then I took the chance and zipped into the laser wash.

Inside the shady drive thru, I enjoyed the relaxation of seeing the cycles of presoak and soap wrap themselves protectively around my car like a soft white cocoon. I watched in amazement at the magic of the dirt being whisked away by the rinse cycle and truly enjoyed the fine mist of the spot-free rinse cycle, all without ever stepping out of my car. I proudly drove out in my pristine car and when I arrived at home, I sneaked it quickly into our dimly lit garage before Eddie could see it shining. Since we lived down a dirt road, a couple of trips up and down quickly masked the laser wash.

Yesterday the car was extremely dirty and I couldn't remember the last time I had washed it. I helped myself to a few crisp dollars from Eddie's bank bag and drove to the closest laser wash. I won't tell you what town I was in, in case you know the owner of the laser wash and tattle on me, but I can assure you I didn't really do any damage to his equipment. Luckily, even though it was heavy 5:00 o'clock traffic, both sides of the laser wash were empty. (I had no idea how important this was about to become.)

I put in my bills and the light flashed "PULL FORWARD." So I did. I must have missed the exact place to stop as the red square sign mounted on the left side of the facility flashed "BACK UP, BACK UP, BACK UP" and I did. Then another red square sign flashed "STOP" "STOP" "STOP" and I did. Then all the parts of the laser wash began vibrating and making their starting-up sounds and flashing a warning green square sign at me that stated in just a matter of seconds "PREWASH" "PREWASH" "PREWASH" would be soaking my car. At about this thirty-second warning I remembered I had failed to remove my magnets from the back of the van. Oh no!

What if the pink one got blown off and some other car pulled up behind me and ran over it and damaged it and I wouldn't be able to declare "Survivor" for the entire world to see? What if it blew off and I forgot to go back and get it and I lost it forever?

I had to jump out immediately and at least save my pink magnet! I could run around to the back and grab it and run back to the driver's door and jump back into the car. It didn't sound like too bad of an idea and what could possibly go wrong?

Well, I could lock myself out of the car by accident and have to explain to Eddie over someone's borrowed cell phone why I needed him to drive thirty miles to bring me my extra set of keys. As soon as I explained the first problem to him I would have to explain why my car was parked inside another man's car-washing facility and that might not be too much fun.

Okay, I could be sure that I didn't lock myself out of the car. I hurriedly unlocked all the doors on my van. I glanced at the vibrating PREWASH wand and realized I had probably wasted twenty precious seconds having thought through the only possibility of my scheme failing. Time to make a run before the laser wash started running around my car.

A little voice inside my head said, "Don't do it, Patty Cakes!" I reconsidered. The safe thing was to sit in the car and wait until the laser wash completely finished and then jump out and run around to the back and see if my pink magnet was on the ground or still on the car.

I thought I had a really good plan figured out. The PREWASH wand started about a foot off the pavement and stood vertically about six feet high. It had dozens of little holes drilled into it so the car wash could clean both short cars and tall pickups. I looked at the wand. How wet could I get? Not too wet if I stayed behind the wand itself.

Since the PREWASH was going to start in five, four, three, two, one second, here it went, I would wait until PREWASH came from the right front fender, wetting the front of the car and then to the left side. When it cleared the driver's door I would jump out and run to the back. I checked the locks again. Unlocked. I put my hand on the door and waited, waited, waited, and then the PREWASH wand wet the driver's door and window and headed to the back. I jumped out and followed it toward the rear, being careful to stay a foot behind it. By doing so I made my first two major mistakes at the same time; one leaving the security of the car and two, leaving the door open instead of shutting it.

Now I was getting a little wet, but I was on my way home for the day after I cleaned the car so it really didn't matter. I made it to the back corner of the driver's side of the van just behind the PREWASH wand. I waited for the PREWASH wand to turn the corner and wet down the back of the van and head on over to the passenger side. I was right up on the wand when it stopped and sat there for a few seconds and then low and behold, it started coming back at me! I was barely able to step away from the van so the wand could clear me and zip; it started back toward the driver's door—you know the door I had left partially open so I could jump back in quicker.

Out of the corner of my eye I could see the pink magnet still stuck to the back of the van. I reached out and scrapped it off with my fingernails and made a mad rush to beat the PREWASH wand to the open driver's door.

To my horror, the wand slipped just inside the opening of the door and while it was soaking the inside of my car with PREWASH, it was also opening the car door further and further. I couldn't think of a way to stop it from pushing the door completely open but as it turned out, I shouldn't have wasted my time worrying about it.

Mounted shoulder high on the building's brick wall was a metal bracket about a foot long. With a loud crash, the metal bracket stopped not only the door but also the PREWASH wand. I saw my car (that I had left in park) move forward a few inches from the pressure of the wand pushing on the car door. Both the wand and the door were applying pressure to the metal bracket. With each pulse of the PREWASH, the car would rock forward a little and then bounce back. Maybe I should take the car out of park so the transmission wouldn't get ruined? But, scared I would make another mistake, I just stood and watched my car door appear to be wrenched off its hinges.

The wand kept pulsing out PREWASH until it finally figured out it was stuck and then an alarm sounded. While the laser wash was contemplating whether to either shut down or call for the police through its security system, I tried to think what I could do.

I had a major dilemma. There I was, covered from head to knees with PREWASH, standing beside my running car, watching the car door being pulverized by the PREWASH wand. I couldn't think straight for the noise of the alarm and then a red square light began rapidly flashing "STOP, STOP, STOP." Duh! That was the problem; I didn't know how to make it all stop!

How to get out of this jam? "Lord, I need some brains please!"

I jumped in the soaking-wet front seat and tried to put the car into drive. Since the car had been moved several inches by the force of the wand, it appeared I was not going to be able to pull the lever down to drive. (My Nissan "space ship" had a round dash with the transmission level mounted on the dash.) It wouldn't budge. I pulled again and heard a thud. The car lurched into drive. I could move it forward!

I mashed on the brakes and slowed it to a crawl. Then I got out and used all my strength to pull on the PREWASH wand. I could not budge the wand. Yet, as the car moved slowly forward, the car door began to close and I pulled again with all my might on the wand. The computer controlling the PREWASH thankfully shut it off and it quit spraying me in the face. The wand quivered a time or two in my hand but allowed me to pull it toward me. The car door closed a little more.

I let go of the wand and jumped back into the driver's seat. Using the brake and then a little gas I managed to drag the car door out of the grasp of the wand. Of course I was also dragging it across the metal bracket. I could hear metal on metal and knew I was tearing up the door but by golly I had to free my car door before anyone saw me! I could just see the headlines in the newspapers: "Car-wash owner's wife loses car door in competitor's car wash." Or worse, see a big yellow wrecker with a big burly man hauling my car, minus the driver's door, to the Nissan dealership. (At least no one would know it was mine since I had removed the pink magnet!)

I increased pressure on the gas pedal and the car moved forward and with a few more terrible noises that only a car crusher could imitate, my door came free! Yeah, I was free! Yes, my car was covered in soap but I was free! I drove so fast out of the stall that I bounced over the exit curb and almost tore up the bottom of my car—but I was free! That was all that mattered.

Rounding the front of the car wash, I heard the miraculous sound of the laser wash washing the air where only shortly before my car had been sitting. I checked the lanes leading into the two laser washstalls and saw no one so I zoomed around the car wash and back into the stall I had just been released from, using my wipers to swish away the PREWASH soap. I pulled into the stall just in time to have half of my car rinsed with spot-free rinse.

When I pulled out of the stall for the second time, my car was half washed and half rinsed on the outside and literally drowned with PREWASH on the inside. I resembled a near-drowned long-haired sheep dog that you see on television being rescued after a flash flood washes through ranching country. But, I had gotten my car out of the grips of that terrible laser wash-wand all by myself! I pulled over in a parking lot and took a good look at the side of my car. Believe it or not, there were only a few minor scratches! I went home with a big smile.

Pulling into the garage with a half-spotted car, I saw Eddie driving up in his truck. I bounded up to him like a wet and happy sheep dog and smiled my best smile as I laughingly tried to explain to him why the car looked like it did. His stern look said that he was having a hard time figuring out why I was so happy about damaging my car and I tried harder to get him to understand my euphoria.

He just couldn't get it! I was bouncing around with a smile, not because I damaged the car, but because I won something! I had been in a very tense situation and had come out victorious. I had competed with a man-made contraption and deprived it of my car door.

Eddie just kept on looking at me in that way of his that says, "She has some loose parts in her head." But I kept on trying to convince him I should be smiling. Finally I said, "Look, Eddie, honey, I've spent eight hours a day for the last thirteen years doing the very best job I could at work and I don't even have one certificate of appreciation for my years of labor. I haven't felt a sense of accomplishment since the last kid went off to college. But today, I actually drove away from that laser wash feeling like a winner."

"But you created the problem to begin with! You should have stayed inside the van!"

"I know, but I created the problem because I stepped out of my protective shell and displayed my love of the Survivor ribbon. A ribbon that represents the greatest accomplishment I've ever made in life besides raising Sharla. Then I solved the problem by using my head and taking control of the situation. I used my brain and my brawn to fight the laser wash-wand for my car door. And when I drove out of that laser wash I heard the first at-a-girl I had heard since you were leaning over my hospital bed and encouraging me to wake up from the surgery to remove my breast. I can't tell you, Eddie, how great that phrase sounded. I would drive my car into that laser wash and do it all over just to feel that euphoric again!"

Shaking his head, Eddie looked at me and said, "You know what I think? I think you need to quit spending all those hours at your job and find some other way to make a living. You need to find something that makes you feel proud of yourself or at least find a job that takes up less of your time. And I promise you if you don't hurry up and do it, we won't be able to afford car insurance next year!" With that, he left to get the livestock fed at the barn.

I thought about what he said almost all night, every night, for two weeks. Then I did exactly what Eddie said to do. I quit! I stepped out with a big smile and shut the door behind me, relying for the first time in my life completely on God. He knew what He had in store for me and I trusted Him to open wide the next door He would have me walk through. I'm not afraid. I'm ready to help where he leads me.

> *If I tell you to go and speak to someone, then go! And when I tell you what to say, don't leave out a word! I promise to be with you and keep you safe.*
> JEREMIAH 1:7-8 CEV

Epilogue

"Call me if you need me, okay? I've got to get back to work." Hanging up, I glanced into the boss' office. Busy with her own work, she probably hadn't noticed I had been on a personal phone call for four or five minutes. Even if she had, it would be okay, as all I had to do was explain that the woman on the other end had been diagnosed with breast cancer.

Just as He had promised, God provided me with a platform from which I could help other women and their families cope with cancer. Several times in the past two years since I came to work at the bank, I was granted time to comfort a woman frightened by what lay ahead of her. Along with counseling, I was continuing my campaign of spreading the news concerning the need for annual mammograms, doing my part in the fight against breast cancer.

My main duty at work was to act as administrative assistant to the president of the bank, second was marketing. It was quickly apparent I didn't have the eye to design advertising, but I was good at promoting the bank in other ways. Wearing my "thankful to be alive" smile along with a shirt bearing the bank's logo, I enjoyed spending time at elementary schools teaching children the importance of saving their money. Plus, as an added bonus for myself, I ended the class by reading one of the mysteries I had written for my grandchildren.

I experienced great joy watching the faces of the children light up with interest as I read the stories.

The community was also pleased with the bank because my employer had made one of my dreams, since I was appointed the town's Historian, come true. By allowing me access to one of the bank's vacant buildings on the main street of Florence, and paying for the utilities and the cleaning of the building, I was able set up a Hall of History for the town's 150th birthday celebration.

It was more fun than I had imagined. The older citizens lent me their oldest possessions, the churches brought historical displays, and the townfolk gathered the few days we had it open and shared their photos and mementos of Florence and its citizens. I made sure that the first display inside the door gave credit to the bank for use of the building.

In one corner of the Hall of History, I put together an old-fashioned bedroom complete with a handmade wooden rocking chair, old Singer sewing machine, braided rug, and antique bed. The bed was covered in a chenille bedspread, with an old wedding-ring quilt at its foot. What made the scene from yesteryear unique were two precious people. One occupied the bed during the days I worked on the displays: Momma, now eight-six years of age and into her "lullaby" years slept peacefully no matter how many nails I pounded or how many people came in and out of the building to lend a helping hand.

Number two was a round-faced little cherub named Thomas Michael Williams. Thomas is Sharla's baby boy, Abigail's little brother, who was born a year after Sharla and Michael moved back home from South Carolina. Now their little family lives right outside my backdoor in their own house. With Michael in Iraq fighting for freedom, Eddie and I are acting as the second parent in Abby's and Thomas's life.

Joining me at the Hall after it opened, Sharla would place Thomas on the old bed and cover him with the heirloom quilt. Visitors would believe him to be a life-sized china doll until someone would exclaim, "It's a real baby!" The youngest and the oldest of my family made the bedroom scene the talk of the town.

Eddie even took the day off from farming and drove us in the parade where we rode in his Ranger, decorated in red, white, and blue in honor of Michael. Later that day, I took a picture of Eddie playing checkers with one of his life-long friends to put in the history box I am compiling to memorialize the birthday celebration. I'll try my best to limit the number of pictures specifically of my family.

No one knows it, but I cried when I removed the last carload of antiquities from the building. What a sweet, sweet daytime dream it had been to provide a gathering place for our citizens to reminisce about the olden days and to play hostess in a house full of the town's prized possessions.

Who would have thought that the scared and frightened bald-headed woman of just a few short years ago would have the strength and most importantly, the backing of a new employer, to put together a display that was enjoyed by so many. A fete that wouldn't have been possible without God's healing hands and the donation of the building and the bank employees who volunteered their time and efforts. Look at all I would have missed if I hadn't listened when God said it was time to do something different for a living.

I love my job. My hours at work are 8 to 5 and I'm not required to put in any overtime. I go home each day with a clear head and don't have to worry about the safety of employees or the problems I had at my old job trying to please seven bosses. With God guiding my fingers while writing several times a week, I finished my manuscript. Completed and sent off to be edited, I declared it a done deal. I started on a book proposal, serious on having it published as soon as possible.

When my boss's birthday rolled around the next month, the farthest thing from my mind was writing another chapter to the already finished book. I made a birthday banner, ordered lunch for fifty people, and spent a considerable amount of time trying to buy something within a working girl's price range for a boss that along with her mother, owned the controlling shares of a community bank with six branches. The morning of the party, I placed my best linen tablecloth over an eight foot table in the administration building and sprinkled a large bag of brightly colored confetti on top.

The party was well attended, the food was good, the cake made by Mandy, one of the other employees, was wonderful, and the boss liked her blouse. When the party was over, I carefully rolled up the tablecloth and placed it inside a plastic bag, trying to limit the amount of confetti that would have to be vacuumed off the floor. My plan was to stop on the side of our county road and shake out the multicolored paper as I didn't want it in my yard or in the utility room at home. Tossing it into the back floorboard of my van, I promptly forgot about it.

Well into the next week, I called my oncologist about an appointment; apparently they had forgotten to send me an allotted time to come back and see him. To my surprise, I learned I had finished the clinical trial that I had been a part of for the last five years: *Congratulations! You've made it to the five-year marker of being cancer free.*

Hanging up the phone, I wanted to shout! Dancing around cubicle walls and interrupting the other thirteen ladies on the top floor who were trying to work, I blurted out my news. "Hooray for me! I'm alive and cancer free. Five years has passed since I was diagnosed and scared to death one hot day in July."

Stopping at one desk in particular, I hugged the lady smiling up at me. Diagnosed with breast cancer three months earlier, Marcella had many long months ahead of her before she could dance to the same beat I was hearing in my head. My role in her recovery was to give advice, if she asked for it, and to give her hope that all would come out okay. Surely my contagious excitement went a long way in giving her confidence to face her tomorrows.

Finally settling down, I returned to my desk and called Eddie and Sharla and made plans to call everyone else I knew at lunchtime. Fidgeting for another hour until noon rolled around I made only a tiny dent in my workload. Grabbing my lunch from the kitchen's refrigerator, I made my way to a secret spot I had been visiting for the last six years on days when Eddie didn't come into town to buy me lunch. It was a quiet place, all my own at the noon hour, as no one had ever beat me to the shadiest spot in town.

Driving into the cemetery from the west end, I reduced my speed and turned south between the rows of weathered headstones. Passing between the granite monuments, I read the names of many of Florence's founding fathers: Atkinson, Guthrie, Caskey, Howell, Preslar, Smart; names I was much more familiar with since the Hall of History.

During our eighteen years of living in this area, we had attended many funerals and burials in this cemetery, two for children of our friends. One was Tom Ed and Billie Jean Atkinson's son, Brian. The other was Bill and Sherry Ellis' daughter, Raven. When I parked my van underneath the two towering live oak trees that shaded at least twenty grave sites, Brian's grave was on my right and Raven's was on my left.

It was a good thing nobody disturbed me at my spot in the cemetery because they would have run to Eddie and confirmed his suspicions that I had lost all my marbles, as I had a habit of talking aloud to the children. Before I was diagnosed with cancer, I would rant and rave between their graves, asking God why couldn't I trade places with them so they could be here with their families. After I came down with cancer, I would ask them questions about heaven, assuming I would soon be joining them. Was it pretty there, Raven? Are you okay, Brian, without your family beside you? Will I miss my family terribly when I join you?

In the past couple of years, feeling that my time on Earth had been extended, I read chapters of my manuscript out loud underneath the huge expanse of the oaks and studied my Sunday School lesson. Sometimes, the quietness of the place softened the tensions of the day and I slept the last ten minutes of my lunch hour. I didn't worry about being late to clock back in at work because I always awoke a few minutes before 1 o'clock. After all, I had friends in high places watching out for me.

Eating my lunch on what I have become to call *celebration day*, I had the windows rolled up and the air conditioner running, as it was a hot outside. Glancing toward Raven's grave, I stopped chewing and sat perfectly still. On the headstone marked *Baker*, right beside my car door, was a lone dove, a female dove clothed in muted colors. She was staring right at me, turning her head sideways over and over again, as if she were shrugging make-believe shoulders and asking me questions. *What? You're surprised that you've made it five-years? Where's your faith? Didn't God tell you He had plans for you when* you left your old job? How many miracles does it take for you to believe that the Old Man upstairs is in control?

It was my very own dove that had visited me twice before! Slowly I rolled down my window, thinking to be closer to her. Hearing the sound of the electric window, she ruffled her wings a little but stayed on the headstone, continuing to look at me. I couldn't stand it, I had to get out of the car and see how close I could get to her. Turning off the motor, I attempted to quietly open my door, forgetting that the hinges squeaked ever since it had nearly been wrenched off by the laser wash-wand. The piercing noise scared her and she flew straight up into one of the live oaks. I got out and searched in vain for her among the limbs for several minutes. But, message delivered, she was gone. Once again, God had been talking and thankfully, I had been listening.

Wow! I was shaking from head-to-toe with the realization that I had been that close to my dove sent from God. Wanting to share my experience immediately, I called Marcella back at the bank and told her. Although she hadn't witnessed the scene, my exhilaration was contagious even over the phone. She, too, was positive that the dove was sent from the Lord.

Hanging up, still heady with excitement, I needed to do something special to celebrate. I racked my brain but couldn't come up with anything. Then the little voice of Patty Cakes spoke up: *What cha' saving the confetti for? Children love a party!* As usual, her suggestion sounded like a good one.

Dragging out the plastic bag from the back of the van, I was as excited as a child at a birthday party. Walking toward Brian's grave, as if on cue, I felt the wind pick up. Glancing down at his headstone, I noticed something I had not seen before. With loving hands, someone had created a heart from small rocks. Careful to unroll only half of the cloth, I lifted it high into the air and shook it hard. Multi-colored dots of paper caught in the wind and traveled the few feet to Brian's grave. Landing gently inside the heart and on the green grass atop his grave, the confetti covered the ground in a blanket of bright colors.

Across the dirt road at Raven's grave, I shook the rest of the tablecloth into the air. Someone with loving hands decorated her gravestone with tiny toy figurines from her childhood. Soon the toys and her grave were covered in dots of color. Standing in the wind, with the tablecloth flapping noisily in front of me, I breathed deeply and let all of the air out slowly. The last remains of the very scary experience of having breast-cancer left my body. Finally, my race was over, one that I had completed with a smile plastered across my face almost every day.

Satisfaction with myself made me smile today, too. My battle with breast cancer hadn't been in vain. I had successfully completed five years of research including numerous types of x-rays, sonograms, an annual ekg, and vial after vial of blood work. All conducted not only to forever scare cancer away from my body, but also to aid other women in the treatment of theirs. Surely, my dove was a sign from God that He was proud of me, too.

As usual, when my emotions peaked, tears followed. Rolling the tablecloth into a ball, I ran my tongue around my top lip and wondered for the hundredth time in the last five years, just where in my body was this never-ending ocean of salty water located? Was their a channel that ran from my heart to my eyes? Funny the doctors had not discovered it with all the x-rays!

Drying my eyes on the hem of the tablecloth, I bid Raven and Brian a fond farewell, promising them that when we met in heaven, we would decorate the white clouds with colored confetti. *Thanks kids, for joining in on my celebration.*

Back in my car, headed to work, I wondered what Billie Jean and Sherry would think when they came to visit the graves of their children. If they discovered I was the culprit who littered on the graves, how would I explain the need to share my joy with their children? Eddie was probably right, a few of my marbles may have rolled away sometime when I wasn't looking.

At home that evening, I stole Thomas and Abigail from their mother and while Abby busied herself watering my flowerbeds, Thomas and I rocked in the porch swing. Closing my eyes, I concentrated on remembering a dream I had the night it was determined that Abby was hearing impaired. It dawned on me that I had misinterpreted what God was trying to tell me five years ago. He wasn't assuring me that Abby would be a hearing child, He was showing me that I would remain on this earth, cancer free, long enough to hold Sharla's second child while he listened to the birds chirping in the trees. My dream *had* come true!

Another person in the family believed her dream had also come true. Although my momma knew full well that Thomas was named after Michael's father, she insisted on calling him "Little Tommy." Knowing that it gave her comfort to have lived long enough to see a healthy little Tommy born into the family, I gave up on correcting her. We two grandmothers were very blessed.

While my eyes were still closed, Thomas, like Abby did so many years before him, reached out with his tiny sausage-shaped fingers and touched my face. Opening my eyes, I stared into his blue ones. He is so beautiful with his fat cheeks and his always smiling face. *Oh, thank you, thank you, thank you, Lord, for allowing me time here on earth to get to know our youngest grandchildren.*

Patty Cakes and the woman she grew into are proud to be a survivor in a world ready to join in their dance. I envision a ballroom full of women gathered to give God praises for allowing them time here on earth to dance the survivor's waltz. *Thank you, Lord, that I can join them and for the lessons learned while wrapped in your protective wings. I pray that by the writing of this book, I have made you proud of the time you have invested in me.*

This dance is yours, Lord. *Bring on the music!*

> *I will thank you, Lord, with all my heart; I will tell of all the marvelous things you have done. I will be filled with joy because of you. I will sing praises to your name, O Most High.*
>
> PSALM 9: 1,2

Printed in the United States
114943LV00002B/1-201/P